Thomas Cook

Cook's guide to Paris and its exhibition, 1878

Thomas Cook

Cook's guide to Paris and its exhibition, 1878

ISBN/EAN: 9783741164903

Manufactured in Europe, USA, Canada, Australia, Japa

Cover: Foto ©Andreas Hilbeck / pixelio.de

Manufactured and distributed by brebook publishing software (www.brebook.com)

Thomas Cook

Cook's guide to Paris and its exhibition, 1878

COOK'S
GUIDE TO PARIS

AND ITS

EXHIBITION,

1878.

WITH PLAN OF PARIS.

COMPILED BY MR. CHARLES MOONEN
(*Under the personal supervision of* THOMAS COOK & SON).

LONDON:
THOMAS COOK & SON, LUDGATE CIRCUS;
SIMPKIN, MARSHALL, & CO.
PARIS: THOS. COOK & SON, 15, PLACE DU HAVRE.
NEW YORK: COOK, SON, & JENKINS, 261, BROADWAY.

[ENTERED AT STATIONERS' HALL.—RIGHT OF TRANSLATION RESERVED.]

CONTENTS.

	PAGE
PLAN OF PARIS.	
Paris Exhibition.—Introductory Remarks	5
Historical Sketch of Paris	7
General Information :—	
Bankers	10
Cabs	10
Cafés	11
Churches and Chapels	12
Embassies and Consulates	12
Metropolitan Railway	13
Money, Weights, and Measures	14
Newspapers (English)	15
Omnibuses and Tramways	16
Places of Amusement	16
Railways	17
Restaurants	17
Steamboats	18
Theatres	18
Vocabulary (English and French)	20
Alphabetical Description of All the Sights of Paris	28
Environs of Paris	75
Paris Exhibition.—Miscellaneous Information	84
,, ,, List of Groups, with the Classes Abridged	88
,, ,, Cook's Boarding House	93
Programme of Paris Excursions	94
Index	96
APPENDIX :—	
Thos. Cook & Son's Travelling, Boarding House, and Hotel Arrangements	99

PARIS EXHIBITION OF 1878.

To the French nation is due the credit of having first realized the idea of collecting together on a given spot the products of art and industry; and thus, by a system of competition and honorary recompense, encouraging further exertions to advancement.

The first Exhibition proper—we do not acknowledge as an Exhibition the merely Fine Art show held by order of Louis XIV. in 1757—was inaugurated during the French Republic in 1798. Some eleven other Exhibitions followed, each more successful than the one preceding it, until that of 1849, which gave results so excellent as to attract general European attention. Then it was that Prince Albert conceived the idea of promoting an International Exhibition in 1851, at which the whole world should be invited to compete. We all know how well the Prince's wishes were carried out, and with what splendid success the enterprise was crowned. Four years afterwards, France called all nations to her Exhibition of 1855; but unfortunately, on this occasion, was not supported as she deserved. Next we had the Universal Exhibition of 1862, which was far from giving the results that were expected from it. Finally, was held the Paris Exhibition of 1867, which failed in a pecuniary sense, although it effected an ample share of good, and contributed vastly to the world's progress.

Then followed the World's Fair of Vienna in 1873, and the Centennial Exhibition at Philadelphia in 1876.

With this short introduction we come to the Grand Universal International Exhibition of the present year, concerning which all augurs most favourably, for never was any gathering of the kind so well responded to, and with so much earnestness and goodwill. It covers upwards of a hundred and fifty acres of ground, and is most admirably arranged and combined for the purposes it was constructed for. Its site is the very best that could have been chosen ; it is of ready access from all parts of the city, and its general planning offers to both exhibitor and visitor the most advantageous opportunities of showing and seeing its contents. As an architectural edifice, the Building of the Champ de Mars has no pretensions. It is a temporary construction simply, and will be at once taken to pieces and removed when its object has been accomplished. But the Palace of the Trocadéro, with its beautiful park, presents to the eye a most attractive panorama, replete with marvels of imitative ancient art and modern suggestion. There figure Egyptian temples, Turkish minarets, model churches and residences, international theatres and concert halls, miniature lakes and cascades, rare collections of every sort—in a word, a complete museum of the most interesting subjects, animate and inanimate, representative of the wonders of nature and of art.

But to enumerate the various beauties, curiosities, modes of amusement and recreation, etc., etc., to be found in both buildings, would demand much more space than we can afford ; suffice it to say, then, that the visitor who passes only a single day in Paris, should on no account fail to see the Great Exhibition, and judge for himself.

Further particulars respecting the Exhibition, showing List of Groups, with the Classes abridged, will be found on pages 84 to 91.

C. M.

Historical Sketch of Paris.

Little authentic is known of the origin of this interesting city, further than that in the time of Julius Cæsar such portion of it as is now termed the *Ile de la Cité* was inhabited by a tribe of semi-barbarians, who had chosen that site by reason of the defence afforded them by the encircling Seine.

After its conquest by the Romans, who made it their headquarters, it gradually rose in importance, and from the period of the Emperor Julian, the remains of whose palace still exist (Palais des Thermes), it became recognized as the metropolis of Gaul, and was accorded especial privileges by its masters.

From this epoch to the advent of Clovis, first king of the Franks, A.D. 496, history makes little mention of Lutetia—the primitive name of Paris. But the latter sovereign having married a Christian lady, was, by her influence, induced to erect a cathedral church, which was dedicated to Ste. Geneviève. Under the same government, more fortifications were constructed, also several houses, thereby adding to the city both consequence and extent.

It was not, however, until the twelfth century, in the reign of Louis Le Jeune, that public buildings were undertaken on an extensive scale in various parts of the town. Where the Halles Centrales now stand, many fine houses reared their heads, and comparatively busy thoroughfares interlined them.

The next monarch to improve the city was Philippe Auguste, who caused the streets to be paved, the works of the cathedral and the Louvre to be proceeded with, and the whole of the faubourgs to be surrounded with ramparts and defences.

Then followed in the march of improvement, Louis XI., who added much to the city's importance. In this prince's reign Robert Sorbonne founded the famous school which still proudly bears his name, and which has served for a model to so many similar institutions throughout Europe.

Owing to the constant incursions of the English during the government of Charles V., the suburbs were enlarged, and fortifications thrown around them.

Not, however, till the time of Francis I., that gifted and chivalrous monarch who reigned contemporaneously with Henry VIII. of England, could Paris boast of those splendid works in architectural art that have given her so much renown, and invoked even for the glorious remnants still extant such universal praise and imitation.

To Louis XIV. must be ascribed a great share in the embellishment of the capital, and the founding of many admirable institutions. He improved the Champs Elysées, established the Institute of France, the Invalides, and the Observatory. He erected the Portes St. Martin and St. Denis, and rendered the Boulevarts a public promenade. In the reign of this monarch the magnificent Palace and Park of Versailles were constructed, the records of the cost of which were destroyed, it is said, with the king's own hands, to conceal from future generations the royal extravagance.

His successors, Louis XV. and XVI., continued the work of improvement. Under their respective governments were founded the Panthéon, St. Sulpice, and the Madeleine, the Place Louis XV. (now termed the Place de la Concorde), the famous Sèvres Manufactory of Porcelain, the College of France, and the Ecole Militaire. They also enlarged the Jardin des Plantes, and built several theatres and opera-houses. The Revolution which followed proved most destructive to the antiquities of the capital; but vigorous reaction took place under the Consulate, and a thousand new architectural adornments marked the era of the Empire. The first Napoleon projected and commenced the

Rue de Rivoli, and enlarged the Place du Carrousel and the Louvre. To him Paris is indebted for her magnificent Arc de Triomphe, the Column Vendôme, several handsome bridges across the Seine, and the designing of manifold undertakings subsequently carried out by his successors.

Comparatively few additions were originated by either Louis XVIII. or Charles X.; but Louis Philippe devoted his best energies to beautify the French metropolis. In his reign the Place de la Concorde was rendered what it now is, the noblest civic area in the universe. The grand old Obelisk of Luxor, once the pride of Egypt, lifts its venerable head over such works of art and magnificence as nowhere else are congregated—palaces, fountains, sculptures, avenues, promenades, and fine prospects. Louis Philippe also constructed the fortifications that now constitute the limits of Paris, and achieved many other works of progress and utility.

Napoleon the Third marked the commencement of an era of improvements, such as neither Paris, nor any other capital of Europe ever witnessed before. Everywhere may be seen the good fruits of his interposition. Superb thoroughfares have replaced the dingy alleys and miserable narrow streets of the past. He has restored, enlarged, and beautified almost every public building and place. He has constructed new bridges wherever they were required and opened all of them to the public free. He has remodelled and restored every building that was defective, and made Paris the most attractive city in the world. In short, he has done immeasurably more for her than any of his predecessors, and must therefore be acknowledged as the greatest of her benefactors.

The reign of the Commune was marked, on the contrary, by a series of most atrocious deeds, and the ruins of Paris too well attest its reckless criminality. But fortunately, under the present Republic, almost everything has resumed its former splendour and attractiveness.

General Information.

Bankers.

Ardoin, Ricardo and Co., 10, Rue Joubert.
Audéoud, Guet and Co., 4, Rue Halévy.
Bischoffsheim, Goldschmidt, 39, Boulevart Haussmann.
Callaghan (Luc and Co.), 35, Boulevart Haussmann.
Comptoir d'Escompte, 14, Rue Bergère.
De Lisle (Th.) and Co., 17, Rue Pasquier.
Drexel, Harjes and Co., 3, Rue Scribe.
Ferrère and Co., 3, Rue Laffitte.
Fould, 22, Rue Bergère.
Gil (P.), 6, Boulevart des Capucines.
Hentsch-Lutscher and Co., 20, Rue Le Pelletier.
Hottinguer, 38, Rue de Provence.
Krauss and Co., 29, Rue de Provence.
Lehideux and Co., 3, Rue Drouot.
Lherbette, Kane and Co., 33, Rue du Quatre Septembre.
Mallet (Frères) and Co., 37, Rue d'Anjou St. Honoré.
Marcuard (Adolphe) and Co., 31, Rue Lafayette.
Muller and Co., 13, Rue Grange Batelière.
Munroe, 7, Rue Scribe.
Pillet-Will and Co., 14, Rue Moncey.
Rothschild (de), Brothers, 21, Rue Laffitte.
Société Générale, 4, Place de l'Opéra.
Tucker (James) and Co., 3, Rue Scribe.
Vernes, 29, Rue Taitbout.
Waters (George), Agent for the Cheque Bank and Grindlay and Co., 30, Boulevart des Italiens.

Cabs.

There are in Paris 12,000 *fiacres* or cabs. These are generally very comfortable, clean, and in good condition; but the horses are slow.

When hired *à la course*, the cabman may select his own

route; *à l'heure*, he must obey the directions of his employer. Beyond the fortifications, and between 12.30 p.m. and 7 a.m., the prices are nearly double. It is usual to give the driver 25c. per hour, in addition to the fare. The following is a table of the *tarif maximum* inside Paris:

Cabs with two seats:	Cabs with four seats:
Per *course* or drive 1fr. 50	Per *course* or drive ... 1fr. 70
Per hour 2fr. 00	Per hour 2fr. 25

Additional Minutes:

5	10	15	20	25	30	35	40	45	50	55
F. C.	F. C.	F. C.	F. C.	F. C.	F. C.	F. C.	F. C.	F. C.	F. C.	F. C.
0 20	0 35	0 50	0 70	0 85	1 00	1 20	1 35	1 50	1 70	1 85
0 20	0 40	0 60	0 75	0 95	1 15	1 35	1 50	1 70	1 90	2 10

Cafés.

From their number and splendour the *cafés* of Paris are one of the characteristic features of the city; and being the daily resort of Frenchmen of all classes, they deserve to be visited by strangers, even independently of the attractions which they furnish for their accommodation, being unlike anything to be found at home. They abound in all quarters of the town, especially in the Boulevarts, Palais Royal, etc., where some of them are fitted up with a splendour of glass and gilding quite dazzling, and often with a taste which merits no little commendation. They are not, however, for the rich only—others, on a more humble scale, are adapted for the working and poor man—while well-dressed ladies without scruple resort to those of the better class.

A Parisian café is supplied not only with the chief French journals, but in many cases with the newspapers of England, Germany, and America. It furnishes coffee of excellent quality for breakfast or after dinner, chocolate, tea, ices, and other refreshments.

On fine summer evenings refreshments are supplied out of doors, and the streets facing the principal cafés, the Boulevarts, Champs Elysées, etc., are covered with little tables and chairs, occupied by well-dressed groups of ladies and gentlemen sipping coffee and ice, while gazing on the sprightly scene of passing crowds and equipages.

Churches and Chapels.

Divine service will be held in English in the following churches and chapels on Sunday:—

Baptist Church, 48, Rue de Lille (Faubourg St. Germain), at 11.30 a.m. and 2 p.m.

Church of England, 5, Rue d'Aguesseau (Faubourg St. Honoré), at 11.30 a.m., 3.30 and 8 p.m.; 10 *bis*, Avenue Marbœuf (Champs Elysées), at 11 a.m. and 3 p.m.; 35, Rue Boissy d'Anglas (Faubourg St. Honoré), at 8.30, 10.0, 11.30 a.m., 3.30 and 7.30 p.m.

Church of Scotland, 162, Rue de Rivoli (near the Louvre), at 11 a.m. and 3 p.m.

Congregational Chapels, 23, Rue Royale (opposite the Madeleine), at 11.30 a.m. and 7.30 p.m.; 70, Avenue de la Grande Armée (Arc de Triomphe), at 10 a.m., 4 and 8 p.m.

Wesleyan Church, 4, Rue Roquépine (Boulevart Malesherbes), at 11.30 a.m. and 7.30 p.m.

American Chapel, 21, Rue de Berri (Champs Elysées), at 11 a.m.

American Episcopal Church, 17, Rue Bayard (Avenue Montaigne), at 11 a.m. and 4 p.m.

A *Salon Evangélique* will be open during the Exhibition season, near the chief entrance to the Trocadéro Palace.

Embassies and Consulates.

The following list will furnish such information concerning the Foreign Ambassadors and Agents at Paris as may prove useful:—

America, 95, Rue de Chaillot. From 10 to 3. Consulate, 3, Rue Scribe.

Argentine Confederation, 5, Rue de Berlin. From 1 to 3. Consulate, 13, Rue Grange Batelière.

Austria, 7 and 9, Rue Las Cases. From 1 to 3. Consulate, 21, Rue Laffitte.

Bavaria, 5, Rue de Berri. From 1 to 3.

Belgium, 153, Faubourg St. Honoré. From 12 to 2. Consulate, same address.

Bolivia, 59, Avenue Joséphine. Consulate, 27, Rue de l'Echiquier.

Brazil, 17, Rue de Téhéran. From 12 to 3. Consulate, 43, Rue du Colisée.

Chili, 54, Rue Monceau. Consulate, 26, Rue de Laval.

Denmark, 37, Rue de l'Université. From 1 to 3. Consulate, 53, Rue d'Hauteville.
Equateur, 7, Rue Laffitte.
Germany, 78, Rue de Lille.
Great Britain and Ireland, 39, Faubourg St. Honoré. From 10 to 3. Consulate, same address.
Greece, 14 and 17, Avenue de Messine. Consulate, 20, Rue Taitbout.
Guatemala, 16, Rue de Marignan. Consulate, 14, Rue Le Pelletier.
Hayti, 9, Rue Portalis. Consulate, 9, Faubourg Poissonnière.
Honduras, 27, Rue Decamps, and 88, Avenue de l'Empereur. Consulate, 47, Rue des Sablons.
Italy, 127, Rue St. Dominique. From 1 to 3. Consulate, 19, Rue Miroménil.
Monaco, 22 and 24, Rue Billault.
Netherlands, 2, Avenue Bosquet. From 12 to 2. Consulate, 54, Avenue Joséphine.
Nicaragua, 44, Avenue Gabriel. Consulate, 34, Rue de Provence.
Paraguay, 10, Rue du Mont Thabor. Consulate, 19, Rue de Grammont.
Peru, 56, Rue Monceau. From 1 to 3. Consulate, 11, Rue de Milan.
Persia, 65, Avenue Joséphine. Consulate, 21, Rue de l'Echiquier.
Portugal, 30, Avenue de Friedland. Consulate, 66, Rue Caumartin.
Russia, 79, Rue de Grenelle St. Germain. Consulate, same address.
Spain, 25, Quai d'Orsay. From 1 to 4. Consulate, 125, Avenue des Champs Elysées.
Switzerland, 3, Rue Blanche. From 10 to 3.
Turkey, 17, Rue Laffitte. From 1 to 3. Consulate, same address.
Venezuela, 32, Faubourg Poissonnière.

Metropolitan Railway.

This line, called *Chemin de fer de Ceinture,* describes a circuit round the entire city, within, and generally skirting, the fortifications. Its construction is very interesting at places; the fares are exceedingly moderate. Trains start from the Gare St. Lazare every half hour, and those desirous of performing the whole tour should book *de Paris à Paris*. The passenger is recommended to get on the outside of a carriage, as he will there secure a good place of observation. Twenty-eight stations are crossed *en route;* the total distance is 37 kilomètres; and the time occupied by journey is 2 hours 22 minutes. A recent extension of the line affords the tourist an uninterrupted communication between the St. Lazare Station (Place du Hâvre) and the Exhibition Buildings.

Money, Weights, and Measures.

The circulating medium of France is very simple, and easily understood; it is divided into tenths, on the decimal system. The coins consist of centimes, sous (equal to five centimes), francs, and napoleons. 100 centimes make a franc, 20 sous make a franc, and 20 francs make a napoleon.

GOLD, *and its value in English money.*

		£	s.	d.
5 francs	equal to	0	4	0
10 ,,	,,	0	8	0
20 ,,	,,	0	16	0
100 ,,	,,	4	0	0

SILVER, *and its value in English money.*

20 centimes	equal to	0	0	2
50 ,,	,,	0	0	5
1 franc	,,	0	0	10
2 ,,	,,	0	1	8
5 ,,	,,	0	4	0

COPPER, *and its value in English money.*

5 centimes	equal to	0	0	0½
10 ,,	,,	0	0	1

The *kilogramme*, or *kilo*, as it is generally called, is the French ordinary weight by which goods sold by weight are quoted. It weighs 2 lbs. 3¼ ozs. avoirdupois; therefore, if you want a pound of any article, ask for a demi-kilo, which is 1 lb. 1⅝ ounces avoirdupois.

The unit of length is the *mètre*, which is 39 inches English as near as possible; 5½ mètres nearly 6 yards; 10 mètres, 11 yards; so if you want to buy a dress the length of twelve yards to take home as a present to your wife, cousin, sister, or sweetheart, you have merely to buy 11 mètres. The mètre is divided into 100 centimètres.

COOK'S GUIDE TO PARIS. 15

Long distances are calculated by the *kilomètre*, as follows:—

Kilomètres.	Miles.	Kilomètres.	Miles.	Kilomètres.	Miles.	Kilomètres.	Miles.
1 = about	$\frac{5}{8}$	31 = about	$19\frac{7}{10}$	61 = about	$38\frac{9}{10}$	91 = about	$56\frac{3}{4}$
2 ,, ,,	$1\frac{1}{4}$	32 ,, ,,	20	62 ,, ,,	$39\frac{1}{2}$	92 ,, ,,	$57\frac{3}{8}$
3 ,, ,,	$1\frac{7}{8}$	33 ,, ,,	$20\frac{5}{8}$	63 ,, ,,	$39\frac{1}{4}$	93 ,, ,,	58
4 ,, ,,	$2\frac{1}{2}$	34 ,, ,,	$21\frac{1}{4}$	64 ,, ,,	$40\frac{3}{8}$	94 ,, ,,	$58\frac{1}{2}$
5 ,, ,,	$3\frac{1}{10}$	35 ,, ,,	$21\frac{3}{4}$	65 ,, ,,	41	95 ,, ,,	$59\frac{1}{4}$
6 ,, ,,	$3\frac{3}{4}$	36 ,, ,,	$22\frac{1}{2}$	66 ,, ,,	$41\frac{9}{10}$	96 ,, ,,	$59\frac{5}{8}$
7 ,, ,,	$4\frac{7}{10}$	37 ,, ,,	$23\frac{1}{10}$	67 ,, ,,	$42\frac{1}{4}$	97 ,, ,,	$60\frac{1}{4}$
8 ,, ,,	5	38 ,, ,,	$23\frac{7}{10}$	68 ,, ,,	$42\frac{3}{4}$	98 ,, ,,	$61\frac{1}{10}$
9 ,, ,,	$5\frac{5}{8}$	39 ,, ,,	$24\frac{1}{10}$	69 ,, ,,	43	99 ,, ,,	$61\frac{3}{4}$
10 ,, ,,	$6\frac{1}{4}$	40 ,, ,,	$24\frac{3}{4}$	70 ,, ,,	$43\frac{9}{10}$	100 ,, ,,	$62\frac{1}{10}$
11 ,, ,,	$6\frac{3}{4}$	41 ,, ,,	$25\frac{1}{2}$	71 ,, ,,	$44\frac{1}{8}$	200 ,, ,,	$124\frac{9}{10}$
12 ,, ,,	$7\frac{1}{2}$	42 ,, ,,	$26\frac{1}{2}$	72 ,, ,,	$44\frac{3}{4}$	300 ,, ,,	$186\frac{3}{4}$
13 ,, ,,	$8\frac{1}{10}$	43 ,, ,,	$27\frac{1}{10}$	73 ,, ,,	$45\frac{5}{8}$	400 ,, ,,	$248\frac{1}{2}$
14 ,, ,,	$8\frac{7}{10}$	44 ,, ,,	$27\frac{3}{4}$	74 ,, ,,	46	500 ,, ,,	$310\frac{1}{10}$
15 ,, ,,	$9\frac{1}{10}$	45 ,, ,,	$28\frac{1}{10}$	75 ,, ,,	$46\frac{5}{8}$	600 ,, ,,	$372\frac{1}{4}$
16 ,, ,,	10	46 ,, ,,	29	76 ,, ,,	$47\frac{1}{4}$	700 ,, ,,	435
17 ,, ,,	$10\frac{9}{10}$	47 ,, ,,	$29\frac{5}{8}$	77 ,, ,,	$47\frac{3}{4}$	800 ,, ,,	$497\frac{1}{10}$
18 ,, ,,	$11\frac{1}{4}$	48 ,, ,,	$30\frac{1}{4}$	78 ,, ,,	$48\frac{1}{2}$	900 ,, ,,	$559\frac{1}{10}$
19 ,, ,,	$11\frac{3}{4}$	49 ,, ,,	$30\frac{3}{4}$	79 ,, ,,	$49\frac{1}{10}$	1000 ,, ,,	$621\frac{1}{4}$
20 ,, ,,	$12\frac{3}{8}$	50 ,, ,,	$31\frac{1}{2}$	80 ,, ,,	$49\frac{5}{8}$		
21 ,, ,,	13	51 ,, ,,	$32\frac{1}{10}$	81 ,, ,,	$50\frac{1}{4}$	...	...
22 ,, ,,	$13\frac{3}{4}$	52 ,, ,,	33	82 ,, ,,	$51\frac{1}{2}$	...	...
23 ,, ,,	$14\frac{1}{4}$	53 ,, ,,	$33\frac{3}{4}$	83 ,, ,,	$52\frac{1}{10}$	...	...
24 ,, ,,	$14\frac{5}{8}$	54 ,, ,,	$34\frac{1}{4}$	84 ,, ,,	$52\frac{7}{10}$	...	...
25 ,, ,,	$15\frac{1}{2}$	55 ,, ,,	$34\frac{3}{4}$	85 ,, ,,	$53\frac{1}{10}$	...	...
26 ,, ,,	$16\frac{1}{10}$	56 ,, ,,	$35\frac{1}{2}$	86 ,, ,,	54	...	...
27 ,, ,,	$16\frac{3}{4}$	57 ,, ,,	$36\frac{1}{10}$	87 ,, ,,	$54\frac{1}{2}$	...	...
28 ,, ,,	$17\frac{1}{10}$	58 ,, ,,	$36\frac{7}{10}$	88 ,, ,,	$55\frac{1}{4}$	...	...
29 ,, ,,	18	59 ,, ,,	$37\frac{1}{10}$	89 ,, ,,	$55\frac{3}{4}$	...	...
30 ,, ,,	$18\frac{3}{8}$	60 ,, ,,	38	90 ,, ,,	$56\frac{3}{8}$	...	...

Liquid and dry measures are calculated by the *litre*, about 1¾ pint. A gallon is a little less than 5 litres. The litre is divided into 100 centilitres. An ordinary French wine bottle contains from 65 to 75 centilitres.

Newspapers (English.)

American Advertiser, 5, Rue Scribe. Daily, 20 c.
American Register, 2, Rue Scribe. Weekly, 30 c.
Galignani's Messenger, 224, Rue de Rivoli. Daily, 40 c.

These are the only newspapers in English which are published in Paris.

Omnibuses and Tramways.

Paris is supplied with 682 Omnibuses and 483 Tram Cars. They all run in connection, and the passenger may claim a ticket of correspondence to go on by another vehicle if the one he gets into does not reach his destination. The system is exceedingly convenient for those accustomed to it, but rather confusing and troublesome to strangers. A special Itinerary of the different lines is published at 2*d.* at all the omnibus stations.

PLACES OF AMUSEMENT.
Mondays.
Bullier. Open at 8. Admission, 1 franc.
Château Rouge. Open at 8. Admission, 3 francs.
Cirque d'Eté. Open at 8. Admission, 1 and 2 francs.
Mabille. Open at 8. Admission, 5 francs.
Opera. Open at 7.30.
Tivoli Wauxhall. Open at 8. Admission, 1 franc.

Tuesdays.
Cirque d'Eté. Open at 8. Admission, 1 and 2 francs.
Elysée Montmartre. Open at 8. Admission, 2 francs.
Mabille. Open at 8. Admission, 5 francs.
Tivoli Wauxhall. Open at 8. Admission, 1 franc.

Wednesdays.
Château Rouge. Open at 8. Admission, 3 francs.
Cirque d'Eté. Open at 8. Admission, 1 and 2 francs.
Mabille. Open at 8. Admission, 5 francs.
Opera. Open at 7.30.
Tivoli Wauxhall. Open at 8. Admission, 2 francs.

Thursdays.
Bullier. Open at 8. Admission, 1 franc.
Cirque d'Eté. Open at 8. Admission, 1 and 2 francs
Elysée Montmartre. Open at 8. Admission, 1 franc.
Mabille. Open at 8. Admission, 5 francs.
Tivoli Wauxhall. Open at 8. Admission, 1 franc.
Trianon d'Asnières. Open at 8. Admission, 3 francs. (Trains every half hour.)

Fridays.
Château Rouge. Open at 8. Admission, 3 francs.
Cirque d'Ete. Open at 8. Admission, 1 and 2 francs.
Mabille. Open at 8. Admission, 5 francs.
Opera. Open at 7 30.
Tivoli Wauxhall. Open at 8. Admission, 1 franc.

Saturdays.

Cirque d'Eté. Open at 8. Admission, 1 and 2 francs.
Elysée Montmartre. Open at 8. Admission, 1 franc.
Mabille. Open at 8. Admission, 5 francs.
Tivoli Wauxhall. Open at 8. Admission, 2 francs.

RAILWAYS.
Chemin de Fer du Nord.
Station: Place Roubaix.

Direct communication with Belgium, Holland, Germany and Russia. Through Mail Services to London.

Chemin de Fer de l'Ouest.
Stations: Place du Hâvre and Boulevart Montparnasse.

Direct communication with the West of France, the Coast of Normandy, Brittany, etc. Through Services to London.

Chemin de Fer de Paris à Lyon et à la Méditerranée.
Station: Boulevart Mazas.

Direct communication with the South of France, Italy, and Switzerland. Through Mail Service to India.

N.B.—Passengers travelling by this line with Cook's tickets will receive any assistance and information they may require from Cook's Interpreter, who attends at the Station daily.

Chemin de Fer d'Orléans.
Station: Quai d'Austerlitz.

Direct communication with the South of France, the Pyrenees, and Spain.

Chemin de Fer de l'Est.
Station: Place de Strasbourg.

Direct communication with the Rhine, Belgium, Germany, Austria, and Switzerland.

For full particulars of hours of departure and arrival, fares, etc., apply to Cook's Tourist Office, 15, Place du Hâvre.

Restaurants.

Paris is indisputably the cradle of high culinary art. The ordinary tables d'hôte convey to the mind but a feeble idea of the perfection to which this art is carried; the " chefs d'œuvre " must be sought for in the first-class restaurants. It must, however, be borne in mind that in one of these establishments the taste of the *gourmet* can hardly be adequately gratified at a less expenditure than 15 or 20 frs.

The traveller should also bear in mind that, at the cheaper restaurants, where he partakes of four or five different dishes and half-a-bottle of wine for 2 or 3 frs., it is utterly impossible that the viands should always be of the best quality. The chief endeavour at such establishments is to provide a varied and showy, rather than a wholesome repast, and they should therefore be patronized but sparingly. The connoisseur in the culinary art will of course avoid the *dîner à prix fixe*, and betake himself with one or two discriminating friends to a restaurant of the best class, where he need be under no unpleasant apprehensions. Even the solitary traveller will exercise a wise discretion in selecting houses of the best class, at which a simple repast of 2 or 3 courses may be obtained for a reasonable sum.

Steamboats.

Small steamers ply on the Seine between the Pont Royal and Suresnes, descending in three quarters of an hour, and returning in one hour and a half; fares 50 c. and 1 fr. The trip is a very pleasant one, the landscape picturesque and animated.

Numerous steamboats also ply between Bercy and the Exhibition Buildings; fare 25 c.

Theatres.

Paris contains upwards of forty theatres. The performances commence at various hours between 7.0 and 8.15, and generally last till midnight. As the hours for opening the doors are frequently changed, the play-bills should always be consulted beforehand.

The theatres present to the stranger a highly characteristic phase of Parisian life, and he should on no account omit to visit all the principal ones. As, however, some acquaintance with the colloquial and slang expressions of every-day life is requisite, and cannot be acquired without a sojourn in Paris of considerable duration, strangers are strongly recommended to purchase the play to be performed, and peruse it carefully beforehand.

The best places are the stalls in front of the orchestra (*fauteuils d'orchestre*), behind which are the *stalles d'orchestre*; those in the pit (*parterre*), and those in front of the first tier of boxes (*fauteuils de l'alcon, de la première galerie*).

It is a wise precaution, especially in the case of very popular performances, to secure a good seat by purchasing a *billet de location* beforehand at the office of the theatre, or at any of the *location offices des théâtres*, in the morning. The visitor should be careful to select a *numéro de face*, and not *de côté*. These *billets de location* generally cost 1 or 2 frs. more than *au bureau*, *i.e.*, at the door, but the purchaser has the satisfaction of knowing that his seat is reserved. Strangers are particularly cautioned against purchasing tickets from *valets de place* and similar individuals, who always hover about in the vicinity of the theatres and endeavour to impose on the public.

In the centre of the pit, occupying the best places, may usually be seen from twenty to fifty shabbily-dressed men, seated in a compact body, and easily distinguished by the simultaneous and energetic concussions of their vulgar palms. These are the *claque*, a hired and horny-handed nuisance under a regular leader, paid to attend and applaud by signal; and perhaps the strongest illustration of the habitual submission of the French to dictation.

Prices of Admission to the Principal Theatres.*

Designation.	Fauteuils d'Orchestre.		Fauteuils de Balcon.		Fauteuils de 1ere Galerie.		Stalles d'Orchestre.		Parterre.		Number of Seats.
	F.	C.	F.	C.	F.	C.	F.	C.	F.	C.	
Ambigu Comique	5	00	4	00	......	......	3	00	1	50	1,900
Bouffes Parisiens †	6	00	......	......	6	00	......	......	......	......	1,200
Châtelet	5	00	5	00	......	......	3	00	1	50	3,500
Folies Dramatiques	5	00	......	......	4	00	2	50	......	......	1,200
Français †	6	00	7	00	......	......	......	......	2	50	1,400
Gaîté	8	00	......	......	8	00	5	00	......	......	1,800
Gymnase	7	00	7	00	......	......	5	00	......	......	1,200
Historique	4	00	4	00	......	......	3	00	......	......	1,760
Italien †	15	00	15	00	......	......	......	......	......	......	1,500
Odéon	5	00	5	00	4	00	......	......	2	00	1,700
Opéra †	13	00	15	00	......	......	......	......	7	00	2,200
Opéra Comique †	7	00	7	00	7	00	4	00	2	50	1,500
Palais Royal †	6	00	6	00	6	00	......	......	2	00	1,000
Porte St. Martin	6	00	7	00	......	......	4	00	2	00	1,800
Renaissance	6	00	6	00	......	......	3	00	......	......	1,100
Variétés	6	00	6	00	6	00	4	00	......	......	1,250
Vaudeville	6	00	6	00	......	......	......	......	......	......	1,300

* These prices are subject to alteration.
† Ladies not admitted to the *Fauteuils d'Orchestre, Stalles d'Orchestre*, nor *Parterre*.

VOCABULARY OF USEFUL WORDS.

ENGLISH.	FRENCH.
On the Way.	En Route.
Arrival	Arrivée.
Baggage—Luggage	Bagage.
Baggage Receipt	Reçu de Bagage.
Berth—Cabin	Cabine.
Booking Office	Le Guichet.
Cab—Carriage	Fiacre—Voiture.
Carpet Bag	Sac de Voyage.
Class (First)	Première Classe.
Class (Second)	Seconde Classe.
Class (Third)	Troisième Classe.
Custom House	Douane.
Departure	Départ.
Diligence	Diligence.
Driver (of a coach, etc.).	Cocher.
Duty	Droits de Douane.
For my own use	Pour mon usage personnel.
Frontier	La Frontière.
Guard	Conducteur.
Interpreter	Interprète.
Key	Clef.
Ladies' Compartment	Compartiment des Dames Seules.
Omnibus	Omnibus.
On board	A bord.
Passenger (on board ship).	Passager.
Passport	Passeport.
Porter	Commissionaire.
Portmanteau	Valise.
Railway	Chemin de Fer.
Refreshment Room	Buffet.
Station	La Gare.
Station Master	Chef de Gare.
Steamer	Bateau à Vapeur.
Steward—Stewardess	Steward—Stewardess.
Ticket	Billet.

ENGLISH.	FRENCH.
Ticket (Return).	Billet d'Aller et Retour.
Time Table	Indicateur des Chemins de Fer.
Train	Train.
Traveller	Voyageur.
Trunk.	Malle.
Waiting Room	Salle d'Attente.
EATING AND DRINKING.	**MANGER ET BOIRE.**
Apple	Pomme.
Apricots	Abricots.
Asparagus	Asperges.
Bacon	Du Lard.
Beans	Haricots flageolets.
Beans (green)	Haricots verts.
Beef	Bœuf.
Beefsteak	Châteaubriand.
Beer	Bière.
Bill of Fare	Carte du Jour.
Bill (The)	L' Addition.
Biscuits	Biscuits.
Bottle (whole)	Une Bouteille.
Bottle (half)	Demie Bouteille.
Brandy	Cognac.
Bread	Pain.
Broth	Bouillon.
Butter	Beurre.
Cabbage	Du Chou.
Cake	Gâteau.
Caraffe of Iced Water	Caraffe frappée.
Cauliflower	Choufleur.
Celery	Du Céléri.
Cheese	Fromage.
Cherries	Cerises.
Chicken	Poulet.
Chocolate	Chocolat.
Chop	Côtelette.
Coffee	Café.
Cream Cheese	Fromage Suisse.
Cream Tarts	Méringues.

ENGLISH.	FRENCH.
Cucumber	Concombre.
Cup	Tasse.
Decanter	Caraffe.
Dessert	Dessert.
Dining Room	Salle à Manger.
Dinner	Diner.
Duck	Canard.
Eggs	Œufs.
Figs	Figues.
Fish	Poisson.
Fork	Fourchette.
Fowl	Volaille.
Fruit	Fruit.
Game	Gibier.
Garlic	Ail.
Glass	Verre.
Goose	Oie.
Gooseberries	Groseilles.
Grapes	Raisin.
Gravy	Sauce.
Greengages	Prunes.
Grog	Grog.
Ham	Jambon.
Hare	Lièvre.
I am hungry—thirsty	J'ai faim—soif.
Ice	Glace.
Kidneys	Rognons.
Knife	Couteau.
Lamb	Agneau.
Lemonade	Limonade.
Lemon	Citron.
Lettuce	Laitue.
Liver (Calves)	Foie de Veau.
Lobster	Homard.
Luncheon	Dejeûner.
Mackerel	Maquereau.
Meat	Viande.
Milk	Lait.
Mushrooms	Champignons.

ENGLISH.	FRENCH.
Mussels.	Moules.
Mustard	Moutarde.
Mutton	Mouton.
Mutton (Leg of)	Gigot.
Mutton (Stewed)	Ragoût de Mouton.
Napkin.	Serviette.
Oil	Huile.
Omelet.	Omelette.
Onion.	Oignon.
Orange.	Orange.
Oysters.	Huîtres.
Partridge	Perdrix.
Pastry	Pâtisserie.
Peach	Pêche.
Pear.	Poire.
Pepper.	Poivre.
Pheasant	Faisan.
Pickles.	Cornichons confits.
Pie	Pâté.
Pigeon.	Pigeon.
Plate	Assiette.
Pork.	Porc.
Potatoes	Pommes de terre.
Prunes (Stewed)	Pruneaux.
Rabbit.	Lapin.
Radishes	Radis.
Raspberries	Framboises.
Ray (Fried)	Raie au beurre noir.
Refreshments	Rafraîchissements.
Rice	Riz.
Roast Beef	Rosbif.
Roll	Petit Pain.
Salad	Salade.
Salmon.	Saumon.
Salt	Sel.
Sandwich	Sandwich.
Sardines	Sardines.
Sausages	Saucisses.
Snails (Stewed)	Escargots.

ENGLISH.	FRENCH.
Sole (Fried)	Sole au gratin.
Soup	Soupe—Potage.
Spoon	Cuillère.
Strawberries	Fraises.
Sugar	Sucre.
Sweetmeats	Bonbons.
Table Cloth	Nappe.
Tea	Thé.
Tooth-pick	Cure-dents.
Tumbler	Grand Verre.
Turbot	Turbot.
Turkey	Dinde.
Veal	Veau.
Vegetables	Légumes.
Vinegar	Vinaigre.
Waiter	Garçon.
Walnuts	Des Noix.
Water	Eau.
Water (Mineral)	Eau Minérale.
Water (Seltzer)	Eau de Seltz.
Wine	Vin.
Wine (Bordeaux)	Vin de Bordeaux.
Wine (Burgundy)	Vin de Bourgogne.
Wine (Port)	Vin d'Oporto.
Wine (Sherry)	Vin de Xérès.
Wine (White)	Vin Blanc.
Your very good health	Je bois à votre santé!

MISCELLANEOUS.	DIVERS.
Bath	Bain.
Bed	Lit.
Blanket	Couverture.
Bookseller	Libraire.
Boots	Chassures.
Brush	Brosse.
Coat	Paletot.
Collar	Col.
Cold	Froid.
Comb	Démêloir—Peigne.

ENGLISH.	FRENCH.
Dressmaker.	Couturière.
Envelopes	Enveloppes.
Farewell!	Adieu!
Fee	Pourboire.
Gloves	Gants.
Hairdresser	Coiffeur.
Handkerchief.	Mouchoir.
Hat or Bonnet	Chapeau.
Hotel	Hôtel.
Hot	Très-chaud.
How much?	Combien?
If You Please	S'il Vous Plaît.
Is it far from here?	Est-ce loin d'ici?
Letter Paper	Papier à Lettre.
Madam	Madame.
Make Haste!	Dépêchez-Vous!
Matches	Allumettes.
Milliner	Modiste.
Miss	Mademoiselle.
Necktie.	Cravate.
Needle	Aiguille.
No	Non.
Paris Exhibition	Exposition Universelle.
Pen	Plume.
Petticoat	Jupon.
Pillow	Oreiller.
Pin	Epingle.
Post Office	Bureau de Poste.
Prepay the Postage.	Affranchir.
Room	Chambre.
Shave	Raser.
Sheets	Draps.
Shirt	Chemise.
Sir	Monsieur.
Soap	Savon.
Socks—Stockings	Chaussettes—Bas.
Stop!	Arrêtez!
Street	Rue.
Take care!	Prenez garde!

COOK'S GUIDE TO PARIS.

ENGLISH.	FRENCH.
Telegraph Office	Bureau du Télégraphe.
Thank You	Je Vous Remercie.
That is too dear	C'est trop cher.
Thimble	Dé à Coudre.
Thread	Fil.
Towel	Serviette.
Trousers	Pantalon.
Walking-stick	Canne.
Umbrella	Parapluie.
Waistcoat	Gilet.
Warm	Chaud.
Washerwoman	Blanchisseuse
Water Closet	Cabinet d'aisances.
Yes	Oui.

DAYS, ETC.	JOURS, ETC.
Sunday	Dimanche.
Monday	Lundi.
Tuesday	Mardi.
Wednesday	Mercredi.
Thursday	Jeudi.
Friday	Vendredi.
Saturday	Samedi.
Easter	Pâques.
Whitsuntide	Pentecôte.
Christmas	Noël.
Spring	Printemps.
Summer	Eté.
Autumn	Automne.
Winter	Hiver.
A Day	Un Jour.
A Night	Une Nuit.
A Week	Une Semaine.
A Fortnight	Une Quinzaine.
A Month	Un Mois.
A Year	Un An—Une Année.
Yesterday	Hier.
To-day	Aujourd'hui.
To-morrow	Demain.

ENGLISH.	FRENCH.
NUMBERS.	NOMBRES.
One	Un.
Two	Deux.
Three	Trois.
Four	Quatre.
Five	Cinq.
Six	Six.
Seven	Sept.
Eight	Huit.
Nine	Neuf.
Ten	Dix.
Eleven	Onze.
Twelve	Douze.
Thirteen	Treize.
Fourteen	Quatorze.
Fifteen	Quinze.
Sixteen	Seize.
Seventeen	Dix-sept.
Eighteen	Dix-huit.
Nineteen	Dix-neuf.
Twenty	Vingt.
Twenty-five	Vingt-cinq.
Thirty	Trente.
Forty	Quarante.
Fifty	Cinquante.
Sixty	Soixante.
Seventy	Soixante-dix.
Eighty	Quatre-vingt.
Ninety	Quatre-vingt-dix.
A Hundred	Cent.
A Thousand	Mille.

Paris.

(Population, 2,000,000.)

Abattoirs.

Strangers should visit these new slaughter-houses, situated in the Rue de Flandre. The cleanliness which prevails throughout is admirable. The number of cattle slaughtered here weekly exceeds 14,000 oxen, cows, and calves, and 65,000 sheep and pigs. A small fee is expected.

Arc de Triomphe du Carrousel.

Erected in the centre of the Place du Carrousel by order of Napoleon I. in 1806, in imitation of the Arch of Severus at Rome, and at a cost of 1,400,000 francs. On the coloured marble columns stand eight statues of soldiers of the Empire, in the uniforms of their different corps; and on the four faces are marble reliefs, representing battles, etc., of the Imperial period. The arch was originally surmounted by the four bronze horses from the Basilica of St. Mark, at Venice; these, however, were restored to Venice in 1814, and have been replaced by a female figure in a chariot, designed to represent the Restoration.

Arc de Triomphe de l'Etoile.

The largest and finest structure of the kind in the world. It stands on a slight eminence, and is visible from almost every part of the environs of Paris. It was commenced by order of Napoleon I. in 1806, on the designs of the architect Chalgrin, but was not completed until 1836. This noble monument is 162 feet high, 157 feet broad, and 72 feet thick. The following groups adorn the eastern front, facing the Tuileries:—departure of the troops to the frontier in 1792; the death of General Marceau; Napoleon crowned by the goddess of Victory in 1810; Mustapha Pacha taken prisoner by Murat at the battle of Aboukir. On the western front:—resistance of the French nation to the invading armies in 1814; passage of the bridge of Arcole; the peace of 1815; capture of Alexandria, where Kléber, who has received a wound on the head, points out the enemy to the troops. The *reliefs* on the northern side represent a somewhat confused group of the battle of Austerlitz, in which the myth invented by French historians of the Russian regiments sunk amidst the ice is not wanting. On the southern side of the building is a representation of the battle of Jemmapes. The names of the principal victories of Napoleon I. are engraved upon a row of shields above the entablature. Under the side arches are 384 names of French generals who fell in battle. The entire edifice cost upwards of ten millions of francs. Nothing of any note is to be seen in the interior; nevertheless, we should advise our younger readers to ascend to the summit, where a most magnificent view of Paris and its environs may be enjoyed. There is no fixed charge for admission, but a trifling gratuity is expected by the guardian. The arch sustained no serious injury during the two sieges of Paris by the Prussians and by the French, but numerous bulletmarks are still observable. In the night of the 20th May, 1871, the Communists succeeded in raising, by steam power, heavy artillery to the top of the platform, from whence they bombarded, with murderous effect, the citadel of Mont Valérien, the strongest of the detached forts round Paris.

Banque de France.

Opposite the Place des Victoires. Was founded in 1800, and since 1848 is practically the only bank in France in the English sense. The capital of the bank is 182,500,000 francs. The building was originally the hotel of the Duke de la Vrillière, and was erected by Mansard in 1620. Some of the rooms retain their original paintings and decorations. The most remarkable features of the building are the vaults, which are of vast extent, and carefully protected and guarded. They can on necessity be flooded, to protect them from fire, or filled with mephitic vapours, so as to suffocate any one attempting to enter.

Bibliothèque Nationale.

Situated between the Rues de Richelieu and Vivienne. This magnificent collection is open daily, from 10 to 4 o'clock, except on Sundays and holidays, to those who desire to study in the reading-rooms. Ordinary visitors are not admitted, except to the collection of medals. Part of this gloomy building was once the palace of Cardinal Mazarin, the all-powerful minister of Louis XIII. and Louis XIV. The number of books (3,000,000) and MSS. (150,000) is so immense, that the bookcases containing them would, if placed in a straight line, extend to a distance of upwards of sixteen miles. Most of the books are copies of the rarest and choicest editions, and are carefully bound.

Bibliothèque Ste. Geneviève.

A spacious edifice near the Panthéon, founded in 1624 by Cardinal de la Rochefoucauld, and which now comprises upwards of 200,000 printed books and 7,000 MSS. Among the former are a considerable number of specimens of the earliest period of printing, when the art was still in its infancy ("in cunabulis"), and valuable series of periodicals from the seventeenth century to the period of the Empire. The library is open to the public from 10 to 3 o'clock, long tables being placed here for the convenience of the readers.

Bois de Boulogne.

This beautiful promenade has become one of the most attractive of the capital. Before the hour of dinner, all kinds of aristocratic equipages and fashionable equestrians crowd to this favourite resort. Here are to be found shady and deserted alleys for those who prefer solitude, and crowded thoroughfares for those who prefer excitement and pleasure. The waters of this park are peopled by water-fowl from all parts of the world. In 1870 a considerable portion of the wood adjacent to the fortifications was cut down as a preparation for the impending Prussian siege. The trees surrounding the lake were fortunately spared, but the bark of many of them was much injured during the bombardment. The northern part of the wood suffered severely during the second siege, and in 1871 the once-smiling *Bois* presented a deplorably battered appearance. The necessary repairs were, however, speedily executed, so that, notwithstanding its misfortunes, the wood still affords a most refreshing and picturesque retreat to the traveller wearied with sight-seeing in the city. To enjoy the Bois de Boulogne thoroughly, the stranger cannot do better than hire a cab and drive to the principal points of attraction, and especially round the river, lake, and cascade. He will thus spend a very pleasant hour, and obtain an enchanting view of the picturesque scenery around.

Boulevarts.

This admirable thoroughfare extends from the Madeleine to the Place de la Bastille, and was formerly one of the limits of Paris. Here stood the fortifications or bulwarks, as its name implies. On both sides it is planted with trees; and the various houses, the splendid shops, the brilliantly-lighted cafés and restaurants, the numerous theatres, and other places of diversion and amusement, combine to render it one of the most lively walks in Paris. At all hours of the day, and until a late hour at night, this promenade is full of people of all ranks, from the labourer to the peer, in search of entertainment and pleasure. In order to inspect the Boulevarts in detail, the stranger is strongly recommended to drive the whole length from the Madeleine to the Bastille. The quietest and most favourable time is the forenoon. When the traffic reaches its climax, between 2 and 5 p.m., the top of an omnibus is perhaps the best point of observation. An evening stroll along the Boulevarts should also on no account be omitted: nothing can then exceed the brilliancy and animation of the scene.

Bourse.

This building, erected in 1808, is one of the purest and best specimens of classical architecture in Paris, and is 212 feet long, 126 feet broad, and 57 feet high. At the corners stand four statues emblematical of Commerce, Commercial Equity, Industry, and Agriculture. The hall of the Bourse is opened at twelve o'clock, entrance free, and numberless vehicles, especially private carriages, soon drive up, and the money-seeking throng swarm into the building. The *parquet*, at the end of the hall, is a railed-off space which the sworn brokers (*agents de change*) alone are privileged to enter. They congregate round the *corbeille*, another railed-off space in the centre, and make their offers in loud tones. The tumultuous scene is best surveyed from the gallery, to which the south side entrance leads. The fearful noise, the shouting, the frantic gestures of the excited speculators, and the eager cupidity of all, produce a disagreeable impression on the mind of the spectator. Amidst the Babel of tongues almost the only intelligible words are: *Je donne, je prends, je vends!* At three o'clock the Stock Exchange terminates, the brokers assemble and note the prices realized in the most recently concluded transactions, and the Exchange-list for the day is then issued and at once printed; but the Bourse remains open until five o'clock for the transaction of other mercantile business. This splendid edifice cost 8,149,000 francs.

Buttes Chaumont.

This picturesque park, situated at La Villette, covers over fifty-five acres, and cost £140,000 to lay out. It is watered by a clear, smooth lake, overhung by a light suspension-bridge. This, with another handsome stone bridge, affords access to a craggy island cut out of the natural rock. The rock is upwards of sixty feet high, and ends in a peak crowned with the Temple of the Sybil, a tasteful belvidere which recalls Rome and Greece, being in imitation of the Temple of Vesta at Tivoli, and of that of Lysicrates at Athens. Though rising abruptly from the very edge of the water to a considerable elevation, this peak is commanded by two hills close to the left, the whole forming unquestionably one of the most romantic sights in the metropolis. These elevations are ascended by winding paths, between green lawns and flower-beds; but neither these nor the bridges, nor the grotto, stalactites, and temple; neither the hanging woodland nor the artistic scenery, are what is most worth seeing. It is the panorama from the heights. There lies Paris, with her glittering minarets and cupolas; there undulates the Seine; there smoke the factories; here stretch the plain and town of St. Denis; to the right, in a deep ravine, passes the metropolitan railway; yonder course the railways to Vienna, Brussels, and London; but where is the horizon? The eye is entranced: within a circumference of forty leagues it surveys three departments, discovering clearly Versailles, St. Cloud, St. Germain, and a hundred nestling villages! But now for the dark side of this picture. On May 26, 1871, the Buttes Chaumont and the heights of Père La Chaise were the two only positions still occupied by the Communists. Those in possession of the park threw great numbers of shells filled with petroleum into different parts of the city, with a view to aggravate the ruin and destruction they had already occasioned, while they in their turn were exposed to an incessant cannonade from Montmartre. On the 27th they were compelled to yield. But in retreating they were met by the advancing troops and entirely destroyed.

Catacombs.

These immense receptacles for the bones of the dead extend some 2,600,000 square mètres beneath the southern side of Paris. The Observatory, the Luxembourg, the Panthéon, and other important buildings, are completely undermined by them. It is calculated that this vast charnel-house contains the remains of at least three millions of human beings. The catacombs once constituted one of the usual sights of Paris; but as they are considered too dangerous, the public are now excluded, and it is a matter of great difficulty to obtain permission to visit them. They form, indeed, a very intricate labyrinth where many people have been lost, and so late as 1871, a large part of the insurgent garrison of the Fort de Vanves met here with a lingering death by starvation!

Champ de Mars.

The Champ de Mars is a vast space of ground extending in front of the École Militaire, and is not without interest in an historical point of view. It was, about a hundred years ago, the site of various market gardens for the supply of vegetables for Paris, and it was afterwards cleared for the exercises of the various troops in garrison. On March 2, 1782, the first balloon ascent of Blanchard took place here; and in July, 1790, occurred the *fête* of the Constitution; the *fête* of the Federation took place one year afterwards. Bailly was executed in the Champ de Mars in 1793; and in 1798 the first Industrial Exhibition was held here; finally, the grand *fête* of Fraternity occurred in 1818; and in 1867, the immense square served for the Universal Exhibition. The whole area of the ground is now covered by the buildings of the Great International Exhibition, which will render the Champ de Mars not only illustrious to posterity as the spot where the world's show was held, but as a sacred soil where the enmity of nations first gave way to friendly emulation.

Champs Elysées.

The finest promenade in Europe. Is divided in two equal parts, and presents a panorama of the greatest gaiety. Upon each side are numerous *cafés chantants*, or open-air concerts, which are open during summer evenings until midnight. They afford the stranger ample opportunity of witnessing one of the characteristic phases of Parisian life. On fine afternoons the central road is thronged with carriages, and the side-ways with pedestrians. Just beyond the Palais de l'Industrie, in the Champs Elysées, is a circular building known as the Panorama (representing the defence of Paris against the Germans in 1870–71), which the tourist should not omit to visit. It is open daily from 9 till dusk, and the price of admission is two francs on weekdays and one franc on Sundays. Two visits to the Champs Elysées, one in the afternoon and one in the evening when brilliantly illuminated, are strongly recommended. During the siege, the whole space was converted into a camp.

Chapelle Expiatoire.

On the Boulevart Haussmann, to the right of St. Augustin. Was erected by Louis XVIII. to the memory of Louis XVI. and his consort Marie Antoinette. Is in imitation of an ancient sepulchre, and may be said to be gloomy without being grand. Its destruction was decreed by the Commune, too late, however, to be carried into effect.

Colonne de Juillet.

A fine column standing in the Place de la Bastille, erected in remembrance of those who fell in the defence of liberty on the 27th, 28th, and 29th of July, 1830. It was inaugurated by Louis Philippe in 1840. It is 164 feet in height, and the figure emblematical of Liberty which crowns the structure is by Dumont. On the sides of the monument are engraved the names of six hundred and fifteen citizens, whose remains are interred in the site of the ancient donjon of the Bastille. In 1848, the killed of February were here interred beside their comrades of 1830; and in May, 1871, the vaults were again opened for the reception of a number of the victims of the Communist reign of terror. These vaults and boats on the canal beneath were filled with gunpowder and barrels of petroleum by the Communists with the view of blowing up the bronze column and converting the entire neighbourhood into a heap of ruins. The combustibles were set on fire by them after their defeat, but the powder had already been removed and employed in the defence of the Place, and the fire therefore occasioned no serious damage. The summit of the monument commands a fine view, especially of the cemetery of Père La Chaise; the ascent is, however, less recommended than that of the Tour St. Jacques, and should not be attempted by persons inclined to dizziness, on account of the swaying motion which is sometimes felt, especially in windy weather.

Colonne Vendôme.

It was erected by Napoleon I. in 1806 to the glory of the French arms in Germany, and is 200 feet in height, by 13 feet in diameter. This column is an imitation of the pillar of Trajan at Rome, but on a larger scale. The total weight of bronze employed in its construction is 1,800,000 lbs., supplied by 1,200 cannons taken during a campaign of three months. The statue of Napoleon which occupied the summit—from whence a fine view of the capital can be obtained—was melted down in 1814, and the metal employed in casting the equestrian statue of Henri IV., on the Pont Neuf. Subsequently, in 1831, Louis Philippe caused a new statue to be cast of the metal of guns captured at Algiers and to be placed on the summit. This was again removed in 1863, and replaced by a statue of the emperor in Roman costume, executed by Dumont. May 16th, 1871, the Commune pulled down the column, to the outer gallery of which the tricoloured flag of France was attached, in order to mark its downfall and the triumph of the insurrectionary red colours. Nothing was left standing but the pedestal, a master-piece of composition, 21 feet in height, and 20 in breadth. But the fragments of the column were fortunately saved, and employed in the reconstruction of the magnificent monument.

Conciergerie.

Forms a part of the Palais de Justice, and overlooks the Seine. This building is most interesting on account of its many melancholy associations relating to the first French Revolution. It now serves as a prison for those who are about to undergo an examination. Queen Marie Antoinette was confined here from August 1, 1793, till October 26, the day of her execution. 288 prisoners were massacred here by the mob in September, 1792. From here hundreds of political prisoners were taken to the scaffold. Here also Robespierre and his adherents were confined a few hours previous to their execution.

Conservatoire des Arts et Métiers.

This establishment is situated in the Rue St. Martin, and is especially intended for the technical education of manufacturers and mechanics. It contains various collections of machines, models, drawings, etc., for the improvement of machinery and implements connected with manufactures, agriculture, and many other branches of industry. This interesting museum is open free on Sundays and Thursdays, from 10 to 4, and on all other days upon payment of one franc.

Cour de Cassation.

Forms the part of the Palais de Justice facing the Pont Neuf. Is newly-constructed on the site occupied, in 1870, by the Préfecture de Police. On the morning of the 24th of May, 1871, the prefect of police of the Commune ordered 150 prisoners detained at the adjoining Conciergerie to be set at liberty. Their joy at their supposed release was of brief duration, for they were now required to aid in the defence of the barricades against the government troops. This they refused to do, and the insurgents at once began to fire on them. The survivors then retreated hastily to the prison which they had quitted, but found it in flames, and thus fell an easy prey to the fury of their enemies.

Ecole des Beaux Arts.

This edifice is situated Quai Malaquais and Rue Bonaparte. The fine arts taught here are painting, sculpture, engraving, gem-cutting, and architecture. At the entrance are colossal busts of Puget and Poussin, by Mercier. Some of the principal *chefs d'œuvre* of architecture are exhibited in the courtyard, those particularly remarkable being:—a Corinthian column in red marble, surmounted by a bronze statue of Abundance; the celebrated portal of the *Château d'Anet*, which Henry II. caused to be erected in 1548, by Jean Goujon and Philibert Delorme, for Diana of Poitiers, his mistress; the arch from the *Château de Gaillon*, which was built in 1500 by Cardinal d'Amboise, Archbishop of Rouen and minister of Louis XII., an exquisite specimen of Renaissance architecture; and many other interesting monuments and quaint fragments rescued from the ruins of churches and palaces. The amphitheatrical examination-hall, the most interesting part of the establishment, contains a celebrated picture, one of the finest productions of modern art, by Paul Delaroche, painted on the curve of the wall, and representing the three great Greek masters, Apelles the painter, Phidias-the sculptor, and Zeuxis the architect of the Parthenon, distributing prizes to seventy eminent artists of all ages and nations, slightly over life-size. Delaroche was engaged four years on this work, for which he received 80,000 frs. In one of the apartments is a fine chimney-piece by Germain Pilon. There is also a large collection of models of many celebrated buildings of antiquity, etc. The Ecole des Beaux Arts is accessible daily from 10 to 4 on application to the porter. A fee is expected.

Ecole Militaire.

A military school, opposite the Exhibition Buildings, commenced in 1752, for the instruction of 500 sons of noblemen killed in battle, and completed in 1763. It was constructed by order of Louis XV., after the plans of Gabriel. The architecture is very fine, and the principal entrance is ornamented with beautiful sculptures. The edifice, which covers a space of 440 mètres in length, and 260 mètres in width, is composed of a vast centre and two wings. Under the centre vestibule are several statues of generals, and in the *Salle du Conseil*, on the first floor, are several fine paintings of battle subjects. At present the Ecole Militaire serves as a barracks to a numerous garrison of infantry, cavalry, and artillery.

Fontaine Cuvier.

A most elaborately ornamented monument, erected at the corner of the Rues Linné and Cuvier during the reign of Louis Philippe, and dedicated to the illustrious *savant*, Georges Cuvier.

Fontaine des Innocents.

This beautiful fountain occupies the centre of a small ornamental garden in the Rue St. Denis. It was built in 1550 by Pierre Lescot, and sculptured by the celebrated Jean Goujon, who was shot during the massacre of St. Bartholomew while working at the figures.

Fontaine du Luxembourg.

In close proximity to the Observatoire. Is a masterpiece of the celebrated Carpeaux, and is surmounted by a terrestrial globe, supported by a group of figures in bronze. It well deserves the tourist's inspection.

Fontaine St. Michel.

This attractive fountain stands at the angle of the Boulevart St. Michel, facing the river, and is quite modern, having been commenced in 1858 and finished in 1860. The central niche, flanked by rich Corinthian columns, is in Languedoc marble. The rockwork, whence the water escapes at the rate of about five gallons a second, is in Soignies blue-stone, and the four basins are in St. Yllic stone—yellow, veined with red. The beautiful bronze group of the Archangel crushing the Demon, upon the summit of the rock, is from the designs of Duret. Two dragons at the basement spout water into the lowermost cistern. The whole monument is 78 feet in height, and 45 feet in breadth. This is one of the most attractive fountains in Paris, and well deserves the close inspection of the visitor.

Fontaine Molière.

This elegant fountain, situated Rue de Richelieu, was erected by public subscription to the memory of the immortal Molière, who died in 1673, in the house opposite (No. 34). The great dramatist is represented in a sitting posture, in an attitude of meditation; below are two allegorical figures emblematic of the humorous and serious character of his plays, furnished with scrolls on which the names of all Molière's works are inscribed in chronological order.

Fontaine St. Sulpice.

Designed by Visconti, and erected in 1847 in front of the Church of St. Sulpice. It consists of three concentric basins, one above the other, over the highest of which are placed statues of the four most celebrated preachers in France— Fénelon, Bossuet, Fléchier, and Massillon.

Fortifications.

In consequence of the blockades of 1870-1, these defensive lines have acquired too melancholy a celebrity not to be an object of interest. They were constructed by the late M. Thiers, in 1841, at an expense of 140 millions of francs. The entire length of the *enceinte* is forty-five kilomètres, and consists of ninety-four different bastions. The ramparts, which average 33 feet in height, are encircled with a ditch 18 feet in depth and from 50 to 150 feet in width. Sixteen detached forts, the most imposing of which is Mont Valérien, "frowning from steep height above," defend the approaches to the city. In 1870, these works were armed with 15,000 coast guns. Owing to the modern improvements in rifle artillery, a series of large forts, planned on the most scientific principles, have been constructed at a much greater distance from the fortifications. Any attempt, in future, to besiege the capital, is sure to end in failure.

Gobelins.

This celebrated carpet manufactory (the property of the State) was founded in 1450, and is situated Avenue des Gobelins. Several parts of the building were burned down during the Commune, and about 75 of the magnificent carpets contained in the show-rooms perished in the flames. The carpets manufactured here are considered far superior to the Persian for the evenness of their surface, the fineness and the strength of their texture. Some of the carpets take as long as ten years to make, and cost 150,000 francs, and even at this high price the workmen are but inadequately paid. The colours and designs are perfect, and the closeness with which the painter's art can be here imitated will excite the visitor's astonishment. None of the carpets are sold. Admission on Wednesdays and Saturdays, from one to three.

Halle au Blé.

Paris Corn Market, situated in the Rue de Viarmes. In 1570, Catherine de Médicis, whose bloody mind was strongly imbued with superstition, erected the Doric column which stands at the exterior of the market, for the purpose of astrological observations. The monument is 100 feet high, and covered with torn garlands, love-knots, etc., emblematical of the widowhood of the princess. At the foot of the structure stood the Fontaine de Médicis, which must not be confounded with the fountain of the same name in the Gardens of the Luxembourg. In 1811, Napoleon I. demolished more than a thousand houses in order to clear the site of the present Halle, which can hold 30,000 sacks of flour. The dome, which is covered with iron and copper, is 126 feet in diameter, and well deserves examination. Two curious staircases lead to the granaries above, which are worth seeing. The visitor, on placing himself immediately under the centre of the skylight over the middle area, and speaking loudly, will find a remarkalbe echo in the building.

Halle aux Vins.

Situated Quai St. Bernard. There is nothing particularly interesting to the visitor in this wine market, unless it be its extent, and the enormous quantity of wine stored in the various sheds, of which there are 444. Some half million casks lie here in bond, the duty being paid on their removal. Brandy and other spirits are deposited in fire-proof buildings. The annual consumption of wine in Paris is 100,000,000 gallons, or fifty gallons a-head on the whole population.

Halles Centrales.

The most extensive market in Paris. It is advisable to pay a visit to this place early in the morning, when all the provincial dealers are busy, and when the variety and style of costume, and peculiarity and difference of accent, cannot fail to strike a stranger. In this great market are united all the various articles

of consumption which supply the town with its daily food—
fish, flesh, fowl, and vegetables. This market has not long
existed in its present condition, and was formerly as celebrated
for its disorder and filth as it is now for its order and cleanliness.
The vaults beneath the Halles Centrales deserve a visit (the
guardian has a box near the south-western corner of the market,
fee 1 franc), and from them extends a subterranean railway,
facilitating the introduction of the commodities into the town,
and the carrying away of rubbish without encumbering the
streets. The market covers a superficial area of almost 30,000
square mètres, and has cost £1,600,000.

Hôtel Dieu.

A large and well-planned Hospital, situated on the Quai
Napoléon, next to Notre Dame Cathedral. It was opened in
1877, and cost 25 million francs. It covers a space of 22,000
square mètres, or 5½ acres. Persons of all countries and creeds
are received here, the only recommendation necessary being
poverty and sickness.

Hôtel des Monnaies.

The Mint is situated on the Quai de Conti, and was constructed in 1771. The front is decorated with six Ionic columns,
and is richly ornamented with carved festoons. The six statues
that we observe represent Law, Prudence, Strength, Commerce,
Peace, and Abundance. The statues which decorate the front
towards the Rue Guénégaud represent the Four Elements.
Twenty-four Doric columns are seen in the vestibule. At the
right we see a superb staircase, well deserving notice. The
principal court, 192 feet wide, and 110 feet deep, is surrounded
by an elegant gallery. The Coining Room merits a visit, and
it may be seen on Tuesdays and Fridays, from twelve to three,
with permission of the Director. The Museum of Medals is open
to the public on the same days.

Hôtel des Postes.

This building stands in the Rue Jean Jacques Rousseau.
It will not compare with the General Post Office in London;
and the difference is very striking at six o'clock, the hour of the
departure of the mails here, as at London. But it must not be
forgotten that Paris has no pretension to being a commercial
city, nor are Frenchmen in general at all addicted to commerce.

The rates of postage for England for letters under 15 grammes is 30c.; newspapers must always be prepaid, and are charged 5c. per 50 grammes.

Hôtel de Ville.

Entirely destroyed by fire in 1871, but now rebuilding. No edifice in Paris was so interesting, architecturally and historically, none has passed through such varied vicissitudes, and none has been overtaken with such utter ruin as this once noble pile. The loss to Paris is irreparable; the value of the property destroyed, including the library of 100,000 vols. and numerous important public documents, is incalculable. The construction of the Hôtel de Ville was commenced in 1533, but was suspended until the reign of Henry IV., when it was completed by the Italian architect, Cortone. Until 1848 it was surrounded by numerous narrow streets, which greatly facilitated insurrectional attempts. On May 20th, 1871, heaps of combustibles soaked with petroleum, and barrels of gunpowder, were placed throughout the building. On the 24th, a fearful struggle began in the Place de l'Hôtel de Ville, and was protracted until the following morning. As the insurgents were gradually driven back, they gave vent to their rage and despair by setting on fire many of the surrounding buildings, and murdering the inhabitants, and two of their number, specially charged with the task, ignited the combustibles in the Hôtel de Ville, while about 600 of the misguided wretches were still within its precincts. The troops, now become masters of the entire neighbourhood, directed a murderous and incessant fire against every issue: no one was suffered to escape, no quarter was given to those who dashed out of the blazing furnace, and no one can tell how many perished in the terrible conflagration. The scaffolding, as it now stands, is very remarkable, and has cost six hundred thousand francs to elevate.

Institut de France.

A classical edifice, on the bank of the Seine, opposite the Louvre, the seat of the celebrated French Academy. The *façade* of this edifice, executed in 1661, forms a half circle, in the centre of which is an advanced portico and the principal entrance. The architect has done his best to give this palace a good appearance, but he has had many local difficulties to contend with, and has failed to give it that air of majesty that one would expect to see in the meeting-place of the *élite* of the *savants* of

France. The Institute is divided into five classes: the Academy of Science; the French Academy; the Academy of Polite Literature; the Academy of Painting, Sculpture, and Architecture; the Academy of Moral and Political Science. There is a public *séance* every Monday, from three to five. Strangers, and especially the learned, will find a visit to some of these meetings of the highest interest. They will have an admirable opportunity of hearing discussions in which the most eminent literary and scientific Frenchmen take part. Access is obtained at these meetings by addressing a written application to the secretary of the department which is desired to be visited.

This heavy monument occupies the site of the notorious *Tour de Nesle*, the traditional scene of many a dark tragedy, and celebrated as being the scene of the infamous nocturnal orgies of Marguerite de Bourgogne and her sisters. The tower has long since been removed, but the spot still keeps in remembrance the horrible crimes and debauchery of former times, and we cease to wonder at the insatiable thirst for royal and aristocratic blood which animated the actors in the Great Revolution.

Invalides.

This superb edifice, situated at the further end of the Esplanade des Invalides, was founded in 1670 by Louis XIV., who realized the wishes of Henri IV., to secure a comfortable home for veterans who had shed their blood for their country. The *façade* towards the river, 600 feet wide, was constructed under the superintendence of the talented architect Libéral Bruant. The insurgent mob of the first French Revolution were supplied with arms by a successful attack on the Invalides. With arms thus obtained the Bastille was attacked and carried. In front of the court extends a ditch, in the rear of which are ranged a battery of trophy guns, fired on great occasions. Some of these are Austrian, captured at Austerlitz, one cast in 1681, another in 1580, with an inscription in German: *When my song resounds in the air, many a wall will fall before me;* some Prussian, decorated with the images and names of four Electors; a Dutch 24-pounder, captured at the siege of Antwerp in 1832; four guns and two howitzers from Sebastopol; two mortars from Algiers; a Venetian piece, of 1708; some Chinese guns; a Wurtemberg 12-pounder, remarkable for its ornaments, etc., etc. The building occupies an area of sixteen acres, and consists of about eighteen different courts, and can accommodate five thousand invalids. The entrance in the centre leads into the *Cour d'Honneur*, to the southern side of which is the Church of St. Louis, surmounted by a dome 340 feet above the pavement, erected by Mansard in 1680. This lofty gilded dome is one of the most conspicuous objects in Paris, and is distinctly visible from almost every part of it; from a distance the basement appears to be formed by the Invalides itself, which, however, is detached from the church. On entering, the eye is struck by the flags suspended from the roof, amongst which the banner which once waved on the Malakoff tower. There is also an English standard, which, judging from its preservation, has not seen much service. The pillars bear memorials of the illustrious generals interred here—Bertrand, Bugeaud, Duroc, Jourdan, Kléber, Lannes, Moncey, Mortier, Oudinot, Turenne, Vauban, and others. At the back of the building, Place Vauban, is the entrance to that portion of the church leading to the Tomb of Napoleon I. Beneath the dome, a circular marble balustrade encircles a depression 20 feet deep, in the centre of which stands the imposing sarcophagus in red marble where repose the mortal remains of the Imperial Conqueror; around stand twelve colossal caryatides by Pradier, symbolizing twelve of his victories. Two winding granite staircases lead down to the vault, on either side of which stand the sepulchral urns of Marshals Bertrand and Duroc. Over the entrance of this vault are inscribed these words from the Emperor's will: "*Je désire que mes cendres reposent sur les bords de la Seine, au milieu de ce peuple Français que j'ai tant aimé.*" Immediately above the crypt rises the magnificent dome, which is adorned with a rich painting dedicated to St. Louis. The faint, bluish light admitted from above, and the sombre aspect of the crypt and its adjuncts contribute essentially to the solemn grandeur of the scene. The visitor can scarcely look upon this marble monument, and reflect upon the mouldering dust of him who lies within, without experiencing some emotion. Napoleon Bonaparte, "the Corsican upstart," with all his faults, and they were many, is yet the grandest warrior of modern times; and however we may deprecate his wanton ambition, and his insatiate thirst for conquest, we must still pause awhile to breathe a sigh of sorrow and compassion upon the soldier's grave.

The *Musée d'Artillerie* should also on no account be omitted. The number of objects contained there at present is upwards of five thousand, for the thorough examination of which a catalogue, which may be had on the spot, is indispensable.

The Invalides is open every day from twelve till three, but the tomb of Napoleon the Great may only be inspected by visitors on Mondays, Tuesdays, Thursdays, and Fridays.

Jardin d'Acclimatation.

This garden adjoins the northern part of the Bois de Boulogne, and is one of the most attractive spots in the environs of Paris. Of the various animals with which this place was stocked in 1870 the greater part were eaten during the siege by the famished Parisians. In April and May, 1871, several desperate conflicts took place here and in the vicinity between the Versailles troops and the Federals of the Commune, and the garden was converted into a dreary wilderness. The work of restoration is now finished, and the park, with its quiet walks, its well-disposed trees, its lakes, and its flowers, the whole occupying a considerable space of ground, offers so many diverse prospects, that it is alone sufficient to attract the spectator; but beyond this the garden possesses many rich and daily increasing zoological and botanical collections. On Thursdays and Sundays, a large assemblage is often collected to hear the musical performances, which are given by an excellent band in an open kiosk. The price of admission is one franc on weekdays and fifty centimes on Sundays.

Jardin du Luxembourg.

The Garden of the Luxembourg rivals that of the Tuileries in the beauty of its design and the number of its statues. It contains many tastefully kept flower-beds and delightful walks. It is adorned by a number of statues and sculptures, placed here during the reign of Louis Philippe, among which may be mentioned the twenty statues of women celebrated in the history of France arranged along the terrace. The grass-plot to the northeast is adorned with a beautiful marble group of Cain and his family after the death of Abel. The central part of the garden is also decorated with numerous statues, both modern and copies from the antique, such as Diana Venatrix, the Borghese Gladiator, etc. At the sides of the large basin, on pedestals of Italian marble, David with the sword, and a Nymph, an Italian work of the sixteenth century. At the south end of the garden is situated the *Pépinière*, celebrated for its collection of 500 varieties of vines, and of roses. The *Fontaine de Médicis*, which stands on the eastern side of the garden, is an admirable specimen of Renaissance art, and well deserves the attention of the visitor. A military band plays on summer evenings twice a week, from five to six. Nine gates afford access to this beautiful garden, which covers an area of 350,000 square mètres.

Jardin des Plantes.

In 1626, Guy de la Brosse, a physician of Louis XIII., prevailed upon the king to establish a garden for the cultivation of foreign plants, the superintendence of which passed into several hands, until 1739, when the direction was confided to the immortal Buffon. His successor was Bernardin de St. Pierre, under whose auspices the animals from the royal menageries of Versailles and Le Raincy were transferred here. Under Napoleon I., a great promoter of the cultivation of natural science, the collections were considerably enlarged. In 1805, Humboldt presented a collection of 4,500 tropical plants, brought by him from America, 3,000 of which belonged to species hitherto unknown.

The establishment, as it stands at present, comprehends:—a botanical garden of great extent and richness; a large and well-planned menagerie; a chemical laboratory; a cabinet of anatomy and natural history; and a public library, containing about 70,000 scientific works. The gardens are open free from eleven to five in summer; and we should advise our readers to see the monkey-house, the lion-cages, the bear-pits, the serpent-house, the hippopotami, the birds of prey, etc., etc., as well as the famous cedar of Lebanon, the first seen in France, which Collinson, an Englishman, presented to the garden in 1734, and which grows near the top of a high mound known as the *Labyrinthe*, at the top of which the visitor will find a pavilion, entirely of cast bronze, with seats, from which there is a very fine view over the gardens, the greater part of Paris, and the distant landscape in the direction of Vincennes and Sceaux. The beautiful botanical garden should also not be neglected. Although these gardens cannot compare with those of London, still they have the advantage of being perfectly free to the public: and the orderly crowds that flock to this place of recreation on all public holidays, prove the wisdom of the rule that opens these places of instruction to the working part of the inhabitants.

Jardin des Tuileries.

This garden extends to the west of the Tuileries as far as the Place de la Concorde. It was designed by the great Le Nôtre in the time of Louis XIV., and although seriously injured during the fearful scenes which were enacted in and around it in May, 1871, has again under Republican auspices assumed its former smiling aspect. It has undergone various modifications at different times, and was originally an orchard. It is separated from the Tuileries by a new street. On every side will be observed fountains, groups of statuary in bronze and marble, parterres of flowers, etc. The bands of the various regiments quartered in Paris usually play here every day during summer from five till six. Sentries at the gates prevent the entrance of men in smock frocks, dogs, and of people carrying large parcels.

Louvre.

Several writers date the origin of the Louvre from the first French kings, whilst others say that it was erected in the centre of a forest by Philippe Auguste, in 1217. Certain it is that the building was not considered as being within the limits of the town of Paris until 1385, when a new enclosure was made by Charles VI.

The palace was originally destined for the reception of foreign monarchs during their sojourn in the French capital. In 1528, Francis I. pulled down the old building in order to replace it by a new edifice, which was finished in the reign of his son Henry II., the sculptures which adorned it being the work of the celebrated Jean Goujon.

A part of the modern structure was erected by the order of Louis XIV.; and it was during the life of this monarch that the superb eastern *façade* facing the church of St. Germain l' Auxerrois was executed after the designs of Claude Perrault. This masterpiece of architecture yields in nothing to the most beautiful productions of antique art.

That side of the Louvre which faces the river is decorated with some most admirable carvings, and the pavilions of *Rohan* and *Lesdiguières* are marvellous instances of the power of the sculptor's chisel, while the innumerable monumental statues which decorate the building on every side are truly worthy of the place they occupy.

On the night of the 23rd of May, 1871, the insurgents of the Commune entered the Louvre and set fire to the premises. Although the most precious *chefs d'œuvre* had been sent to Brest for safety before the siege of 1870, a valuable collection, comprising upwards of 90,000 volumes and a number of rare and interesting MSS., was entirely destroyed by the flames.

The galleries contain various exhibitions, and each one merits the special attention of the visitor. Of course it would be impossible, in the space at our command, to give a detailed list of the treasures of this collection, and we recommend our readers to provide themselves with an official catalogue, which may be purchased in the building.

The first thing that strikes the stranger is the splendour of the decorated ceilings, the work of celebrated painters. Upon the ground floor are the museums of ancient and modern sculptures; the Egyptian, Syrian, Algerian, and Mexican collections, etc. On the first floor are exhibited the paintings of various schools; enamels and bronzes; Grecian, Roman, Etruscan, and Egyptian antiquities; drawings and engravings. The second floor is occupied by the marine museum, a sight which should not be neglected, as showing the progress of the naval art through many centuries; the American museum, consisting of antiquities discovered chiefly in the sepulchres of Peru, Bolivia, and Mexico; sculptures in a very barbarous styles; statues of divinities, hideous in looks, etc.; and farther on three rooms containing Chinese objects, mostly brought to Paris after the last Chinese war, and many of them from the plunder of the royal palace near Pekin. The museums of the Louvre are opened daily, except Mondays, from ten to four. The visitor is recommended to go as early as possible, as the different collections, and especially the picture-galleries, are often crowded in the afternoon.

Luxembourg.

The Luxembourg was begun in 1612 by Marie de Médicis, widow of Henry IV., who had purchased the land from the Duke de Luxembourg; the palace was completed in the short space of six years. Jacques Desbrosses was the architect, and produced a building partly classical, partly Renaissance, in a style of rustication peculiar to itself, and not unpicturesque. The clock-tower, adorned with allegorical figures by Pradier, is of the reign of Louis Philippe. Marie de Médicis left it to her second son, Gaston de France, Duke d'Orléans, from whom it came into the possession of his daughter. It was afterwards the scene of some of the orgies which disgraced the life of the Regent's daughter. Louis XVI. gave it to his brother the Count de

Provence, subsequently Louis XVIII., who inhabited it until the expulsion of the royal family. It was then used as a prison, in which Hébert, Camille Desmoulins, Danton, the artist David, Joséphine Beauharnais, and others, were confined. In 1795 it became the Palace of the Directory. During the First Empire the palace was occupied by the Senate, a legislative body which answers to our House of Lords. Under the Restoration, Louis Philippe, and Napoleon III., it was used as the place of meeting of the Chamber of Peers. It now contains the offices of the Prefecture of the Seine. The Luxembourg was saved from the Communists by the arrival of the troops when they were setting fire to it. Since 1818 the north side has been converted into picture-galleries, which are open every day, except Monday, from 10 to 4. They contain the works of contemporary French artists, or of those who have not been dead more than ten years. After the Louvre, the collection of the Luxembourg is the most interesting in Paris; but as it is necessarily less extensive than the former, a single visit will suffice.

Madeleine.

This splendid edifice was commenced in the reign of Louis XV. The Revolution found the building incompleted, and the works were suspended. It was restored to the uses of religion during the Restoration, and was completed in 1842. The carvings over the entrance in front are from the chisel of Lemaire, and represent the Last Judgment. The exterior of the edifice, with its fifty-two columns and its square form, rather resembles a Greek temple than a Catholic church. The niches in the walls contain statues of saints especially revered in France, all by modern sculptors. The church is approached by a flight of twenty-eight steps, occupying the entire breadth of the edifice. The bronze doors are adorned with illustrations of the ten commandments, designed by Triqueti, and deserve especial notice. The interior is gorgeously gilded and ornamented with paintings by the most celebrated contemporary artists. Notice should be taken of the grand altar, the two handsome vases for holy water, the fonts, and the groups by Rude and Pradier. The light is unfortunately insufficient to display these fine groups to advantage. When the principal door and gate are closed, access may be obtained by the entrances on the eastern and western sides of the church.

In May, 1871, the insurgents had constructed one of their

most formidable barricades across the Rue Royale, opposite to, and within a short distance of, the Madeleine. The appalling scene enacted here on May 22nd and 23rd baffles description. The houses in the Rue Royale which escaped destruction by fire were literally riddled with shells and bullets, but the church, owing to its massive construction, suffered comparatively little. This fearful battle ended in the Versailles army driving the Communists, after much loss on both sides, from their barricade. Three hundred of the insurgents, closely pursued by their enemies, sought refuge in the sacred edifice; the troops soon forced an entrance, and suffered not one of their victims to escape alive.

Ministère des Affaires Etrangères.

The Ministry of Foreign Affairs is an Italian or Classical building, with a very profusely sculptured front towards the river. The first stone of this palace was laid by M. Guizot, the prime minister, in 1845, and the expenses amounted to five millions of francs. The collection of archives and state-papers is very extensive. This monument was struck in different places by projectiles during the sieges of 1870-71; and on May 22nd, a part of it was entirely gutted by the fire, while the remainder was seriously damaged.

Morgue.

A very low, white building at the end of the island of La Cité, at the back of Notre Dame. In this lugubrious building are exposed the bodies of those unfortunates who are found in the Seine or elsewhere. We should advise our readers to abstain from visiting this gloomy place, unless they possess tolerably strong nerves, as the objects exhibited here are sometimes in the very last stage of corruption. Each corpse is exposed for recognition during three days, and there are usually several at a time stretched upon the marble slabs, with a stream of water trickling over them. Of how many sad histories this quiet building has witnessed the closing scene is not within our province to speak; suffice it to say that the many discovered and undiscovered tragedies which it has been the indirect means of making public would fill a volume, and the stranger can scarcely issue from its portals without a reflection upon the uncertainty of life.

Musée de Cluny.

One of the most interesting museums in Paris, situated Rue du Sommerard. It was built in 1490 by Jacques d'Amboise, Abbot of Cluny, and it served for some time as the residence of Mary, sister of Henri VIII. of England, and widow of Louis XII. The wedding of James V. of Scotland with the daughter of Francis I. was celebrated here in 1536. Several other historical personages afterwards made it their town residence. In 1790 it became national property, and was ceded to a private gentleman, M. du Sommerard, who purchased it in 1833, and placed many curiosities in it. Upon the death of that learned antiquarian, the building and the collection were bought by the City for £20,000. Here may be seen some very valuable specimens of antique furniture, arms, sculptures, etc., which curiously illustrate the manners and usages of remote epochs. The Museum is open free daily (except Mondays) from 11 till 4, to strangers provided with a passport or visiting-card. The catalogue, which may be purchased at the entrance, is indispensable for those who desire to make themselves acquainted with all the objects of attraction in this splendid collection, as the number of interesting reminiscences is so great as to defy enumeration here. This remarkable edifice was providentially saved from destruction in May, 1871, the troops having surprised the Panthéon before the Communists could spring their mines, which were destined to blow up the whole quarter.

Notre Dame.

Notre Dame, certainly the finest church in Paris, was completed in 1185, and is built in the form of a Latin cross, The two massive square towers, connected by a beautiful open arcade, are 264 feet in height. In the southern hangs the great bell called the *Bourdon*, weighing seventeen tons. The view from the top is very good, and commands a prospect of the course of the Seine with its numerous bridges. Entrance on the north-western side, for which a trifling gratuity is expected. The treasure of Notre Dame was despoiled during the great Revolution, and the church was designated the "Temple of Reason." The chapels, thirty-seven in number, are ornamented by some very remarkable sculptures and paintings. On the southern side of the church stood the Archbishop's Palace, destroyed by the mob in 1831. The site is now occupied by the

Sacristie, a modern Gothic structure of considerable elegance, and well worth a visit. Here are shown magnificent sets of costly priests' vestments, coronation relics of Napoleon, church-plate—amongst which the ostensoir of St. Louis—croziers, mitres, crosses, etc., many of them gorgeously decorated with precious stones, the cross worn by St. Vincent de Paul when attending on Louis XIII.'s last moments, a cast from the face of Archbishop Affre, and the bullet with which he was shot, and the blood-stained robes of the last three successive archbishops of Paris—Affre, Sibour, and Darboy. Among the relics are two thorns from the crown of the Saviour, and one of the nails of the cross. The interior of the cathedral presents a most magnificent view, and the

"Storied windows, richly dight,
Casting a dim religious light,"

cannot fail to impress the stranger, of whatever creed, with a sense of solemnity and awe. The admirable restorations, which have cost several millions of francs, show us the architecture of the ancient cathedral as it has been so admirably described to us by Victor Hugo in his popular romance. The Cathedral of Notre Dame can hold 21,000 persons.

Observatoire.

The Observatory was commenced in 1667 under the direction of Claude Perrault, who employed neither iron nor wood in its construction. The four sides of the building correspond to the cardinal points of the compass. The great dome on the roof contains a gigantic equatorial hitherto used to little purpose. There is a very fine view from the roof over Paris and its environs. On the floor of one of the rooms will be seen a line indicating the meridian of Paris. The interior is divided into chambers appropriated to meteorological labours, and here may be seen a splendid collection of modern telescopes and astronomical instruments. Strangers are allowed to visit the establishment in detail upon the presentation of a ticket (easily obtainable from the Director), and can hear an explanation, if required, of the utility of the different instruments.

Opéra.

This wonderful monument, worthy of the artistic purpose to which it is devoted, was commenced in 1861 from a design by

Garnier, and inaugurated in 1875. Its estimated cost, sixteen millions of francs, reached upwards of sixty millions before it was completed. It is profusely decorated with marbles, busts of celebrated composers, bronze statues, and four sculptured groups, executed in a most elaborate way. The interior is of such a grand and sumptuous character, that its description is simply impossible. Let the stranger, therefore, go there in the evening: he will find the effect magical. The building is fireproof, iron supplying the place of timber. It narrowly escaped destruction in 1871, when it was used by the Communists as a magazine for gunpowder and other munitions of war.

Palais Bourbon.

The Palais Bourbon, or Palace of the Legislative Body during the empire, faces the Pont de la Concorde. It was commenced in 1772, after the designs of Girardini, and was continued by Mansard. It was originally destined to serve as the residence of the Duchess de Bourbon, and was afterwards acquired by the Prince de Condé, who considerably enlarged it at a cost of twenty million francs. Napoleon I. ordered the construction of a new and handsome portico—one of the great ornaments of Paris—in order to give the building a nobler aspect as seen from the Seine. At the exterior are the statues of Sully, Colbert, l'Hôpital, and d'Aguesseau, besides several other figures, some allegorical, some historical. The interior consists of lofty halls and passages, adorned with statues and *bas reliefs*. The special objects of interest in this structure are: the *Salle de la Paix*, with the walls and ceilings painted by Horace Vernet, and several copies of antiques; the *Salle du Trône*, painted by Delacroix; the *Salle des Conférences*, with many historical paintings by Heim; the *Salle des Pas Perdus*, ceiling by Vernet; the *Salle du Corps Législatif*, or ancient chamber of deputies, in the form of a Greek theatre, surrounded by Ionic columns, and lighted from above; and the *Bibliothèque*, of nearly 200,000 volumes, besides innumerable documents relative to the legislature of France, etc.

Palais du Conseil d'Etat.

On the Quai d'Orsay. Was burnt down by the Commune, with all the valuable records, on May 23rd, 1871. The sight from the river was most horrible, and little more than the external walls survived the terrible conflagration. Now, the ruins present a grand, but sinister, aspect, not easily to be forgotten.

Palais de l'Elysée.

Erected in 1718, in the Faubourg St. Honoré, for the residence of Madame de Pompadour, the mistress of Louis XV. It afterwards became the property of the State. During the "Hundred Days," in 1815, it was occupied by Napoleon I. After the battle of Waterloo it was inhabited by the Duke of Wellington and the Emperor Alexander. Here it was that, on the night of December 1st, 1851, Louis Napoleon plotted the *coup d'état*, which took place on the following day. In 1855, Her Majesty Queen Victoria dined here; and in 1867, the Sultan of Turkey, the Emperors of Austria and Russia, and other princes, resided here. The palace is now the official residence of Marshal de MacMahon, Duke de Magenta, President of the French Republic.

Palais de l'Industrie.

Is situated in the Champs Elysées, and is the most considerable of the modern edifices of Paris, although by no means the most pleasing. Was used in 1855 for the great International Exhibition. On the outside are busts of celebrated men of every country, the French, of course, preponderating. The figures upon the summit of the chief entrance represent Industry distributing laurel crowns, and are very fine. Exhibitions of Fine Arts, etc., take place here annually.

Palais de Justice.

The Palace of Justice, on the Boulevart du Palais, was formerly the residence of the French kings until the reign of Philippe Le Bel, who abandoned it to the Officers of Justice. The greater number of the chambers were built by this monarch. It is now entirely devoted to the administration of the law, and here have been tried some of the most celebrated cases in the history of French legislation. The large square tower at the corner is the *Tour de l'Horloge*, one of the most splendid specimens of ancient architecture. The statue of Malesherbes, the faithful defender of Louis XVI., stands in a niche on the right side of the *Salle des Pas Perdus*, where judges and advocates in their black robes are usually seen pacing up and down. The different courts of justice hold their sessions in the Palais de Justice from 11 till 3 o'clock, and may be visited by those who desire to witness the proceedings of a

French tribunal. In the *Chambre Correctionelle* very amusing scenes sometimes occur, and the pleading is often admirable; the stranger, however, who is well acquainted with the French language, should visit one of the courts in which a civil suit is being tried, and where he will hear some of the most eminent advocates plead. The eloquence of the French *Barreau* is held in high repute. Under the Communist regime in 1871, the *Procureur* of the Commune established himself at first in the *Cour de Cassation*, and afterwards in the *Salle des Appels Correctionels*, where the *sergents de ville* of the Empire, arrested on March 18th, were condemned by a mock tribunal to be shot. On the morning of May 22nd, the *Procureur* ordered petroleum to be poured out in different parts of the palace and set on fire. Owing to these preparations the fire spread with fearful rapidity, and before the close of the day the greater part of the palace was reduced to a heap of ruins.

Palais de la Légion d'Honneur.

A building, on the Quai d'Orsay, in no way remarkable either for size or appearance, but curious on account of its history. It was built for the Prince de Salm, who was beheaded in 1792. It was afterwards put up in a lottery by the government, and was won by a journeyman barber, who disposed of it to a clever swindler who lived here for some time in great state as the Marquis de Boisregard. He was subsequently sent to the galleys for forgery. During the Directorate the building became the property of the celebrated Madame de Staël; but being purchased by the State, it has been occupied since 1802 by the Chancellorship of the Legion of Honour, an institution created by Napoleon I. to reward military and civil merit. Two of the sons of the King of Prussia lodged here in 1814. This construction, which is opposite to the Pont de Solférino, inscribed with the names of the victories gained in the Crimea, shared the same fate as the edifice just mentioned, the expense of restoring it having amounted to 1,500,000 francs.

Palais Royal.

Cardinal Richelieu was the first who commenced the building of this palace, in 1629, and it was originally called the Palace of the Cardinal. Few edifices have suffered so many changes, and the architect would have great difficulty in recognizing his work at the present day. The garden is in the centre of the building, and is in a parallelogram form; a fountain stands in the middle, and there is a double row of trees round it. The covered promenade is very convenient during rainy weather, and here may be purchased jewellery of every description. We should advise our readers not to forget their friends at home while lounging along this attractive arcade, as all kinds of presents for sweethearts, wives, or friends may be obtained here at a fair price.

The historical associations connected with the Palais Royal would fill a volume; suffice it to say that its former reputation was anything but creditable, and here was the scene of the Regent's celebrated suppers and the intrigues of Philippe Egalité, the Duke d'Orléans. The Palais Royal was also celebrated for its gambling-houses and hells. A military band usually plays between five and six o'clock on fine evenings in the middle of the garden. On May 22nd, 1871, the Communists set the Palais Royal on fire, and the entire south wing, including most of the apartments in the *Cour d'Honneur*, with the exception of the south-western corner, became a prey to the flames, and was almost entirely destroyed. Had the galleries, with their attractive shops, been destroyed, the loss would have been incalculable.

Palais des Thermes.

The Palais des Thermes is united to the Musée de Cluny, and is the oldest structure in Paris. These antique ruins, the origin of which is attributed to the Roman Emperor Constantius, who resided at Paris about the year 292, are of great interest to archæologians. The garden contains, amongst other curiosities, a statue of the Emperor Julian, the iron cross taken from the church of St. Vladimir, at Sebastopol, and the Gothic *façade* of the college of Bayeux, which stood in this quarter of Paris.

Panthéon.

The Panthéon, or Church of Ste. Geneviève, occupies one of the most elevated situations in Paris. The first stone of this temple, constructed after the designs of Soufflot, was laid in 1764. The cost of the building amounted to thirty million francs. In 1791, the National Assembly determined that Ste. Geneviève should be called the Panthéon, and serve as a sepulchre to those citizens who had deserved well of their country. Hence the inscription placed upon its frontispiece: "AUX GRANDS HOMMES LA PATRIE RECONNAISSANTE." Although cruciform in shape, this magnificent structure hardly possesses an ecclesiastical character. The form is nearly that of St. Peter's in Rome and St. Paul's in London, but inferior in size. The height from the pavement to the top of the dome is 281 feet. The portico, which is approached by a flight of eleven steps, occupying the entire breadth of the edifice, is supported by a triple row of handsome Corinthian columns, sixty-four feet in height, and six feet in diameter. The pediment above the portico contains a fine group by David d'Angers, the principal figure of which represents France in the act of distributing garlands to her sons. To the left, under the protection of Liberty, several illustrious civilians are represented: Malesherbes, Mirabeau, Monge, and Fénelon; then Manuel, the orator; Carnot, the celebrated general of engineers, and leader of the wars of the First Revolution; Berthollet, the chemist, and Laplace, the astronomer. A second row consists of the painter David, Cuvier, Lafayette, Voltaire, Rousseau, and the physician Bichat. To the right, besides a figure emblematic of History, are soldiers of the Republic and of the Empire, among them Napoleon Bonaparte, as leader of the Italian army; behind him a stern old grenadier leaning on his musket, emblematic of Service. In front of the entrance are two groups in sandstone, representing Ste. Geneviève disarming the anger of Attila, the leader of the Huns, and thereby saving Paris from devastation, and the baptism of the Franconian king Clovis by St. Rémi. The interior consists of a spacious rotunda, flanked by a gallery supported by Corinthian columns. There are three altars in the choir and transepts, all magnificently gilt and ornamented. In the left transept is the staircase leading to the dome, a majestic piece of architecture terminating in a lantern, and surrounded by a gallery and balustrade. The interior of the dome is first reached by 328 steps. The visitor will here have an opportunity of inspecting the painting of the Cupola, by Gros, executed in 1824, for which the artist received a remuneration of 100,000 frs., and was created a baron by Charles X. A farther ascent of ninety-four steps leads to the gallery, which commands a most magnificent and extensive view.

Underneath the church is a vast series of vaults, some of the stones of which are fifty feet in length. The monuments and funeral urns are arranged like the Roman tombs at

Pompeii. A remarkably loud echo may be awakened in the centre of these subterraneous passages by the faintest sound. Mirabeau was the first whose remains were deposited here, in 1791. Near him was placed Marat, the most furious of the Jacobins, who fell July 13, 1793, by the hand of Charlotte Corday. Subsequently, however, both the bodies were removed by order of the Convention; Mirabeau was buried in the cemetery of Père La Chaise, whilst the remains of Marat were ignominiously cast into the sewers. About the same period monuments were erected here to Voltaire and Rousseau. Both these tombs are, however, empty, the remains of the two celebrated writers having been secretly removed during the Restoration, and interred in some unknown spot. Opposite to the tomb of Voltaire is that of Soufflot, the architect of the church. A cenotaph to the memory of the Dutch admiral De Winter will also be observed. Napoleon I. caused several of the most eminent men of his time to be buried here; among others may be mentioned Lagrange, the mathematician, and Bougainville, the circumnavigator. In 1848, the Panthéon was one of the headquarters of the insurgents, and was obstinately defended during two days against the attacks of the troops. During the Prussian bombardment of 1871, several shells, fired from the formidable stronghold of Châtillon, pierced right through the dome.

Parc Monceau.

This beautiful garden, situated between the Avenue de la Reine Hortense and the Boulevart Malesherbes, is one of the most delightful promenades of Paris, and affords a pleasant retreat to those who desire to escape from the heat and bustle of the town. It was designed in 1778 by Carmontel for the financier Grimod de la Regnière, and was afterwards sold to the Duke d'Orléans. Napoleon gave the domain to Cambacérès, who relinquished it on account of the expense it entailed. Louis XVIII. restored it to the Orleans family, who preserved it until the decree of January 12, 1852. Since 1860 it has become public property, and attracts numerous visitors, thanks to the various facilities for reaching it. The garden is not so large as formerly, but all the ruins, rocks, statues, cascades, broken columns, pyramids, etc., which ornamented the ancient park, are still preserved.

Père La Chaise.

" The dead—the honoured dead are here—
For whom, behind the sable bier,
Through many a long-forgotten year,
Forgotten crowds have come,
With solemn step and falling tear,
Bearing their brethren home.

" Beneath these boughs, athwart this grass,
I see a dark and moving mass,
Like Banquo's shades across the glass,
By wizard hands displayed ;
Stand back, and let these hearses pass
Along the trampled glade."

This celebrated burial-ground was laid out in 1804, upon the ancient domain of Mont Louis, which Louis XIV. had given to the Jesuits, of whom *Père* or Father La Chaise was the superior. The cemetery covers 212 acres, and here may be seen the tombs of—

Abailard and Héloïse.
Aboville, General.
Aguado, financier.
Allonville, General.
Andrianoff, dancer.
Arago, astronomer.
Auber, composer.
Balzac, novelist.
Baroche, minister.
Barras, President of the Directory.
Bassano, Duke de, minister.
Beaujour, Félix de.
Beaumarchais, Count de, author.
Béclard, minister.
Belliard, General.
Béranger, poet.
Bernardin de St. Pierre, author.
Boïeldieu, composer.
Boode, merchant of Amsterdam.
Bory de St. Vincent, archæologist.
Brongniart, mineralogist.
Bruat, Admiral.
Cambacérès, second consul, 1801.
Cartellier, sculptor.
Caulaincourt, Duke de Vicenze, minister.
Champollion, archæologist.
Chappe, inventor of telegraph.
Chasseloup Laubat, minister.
Chérubini, composer.

Chopin, musician.
Clarke, Marshal.
Colbert, Admiral.
Constant, Benjamin, orator.
Cottin, Madame, authoress.
Cousin, Victor, philosopher.
Couteaux, captain of engineers.
Cuvier, naturalist.
David d'Angers, sculptor.
David, Louis, painter, President of Convention.
Davoust, Marshal.
Decrès, Admiral.
Delacroix, Eugène, painter.
Delambre, astronomer.
Delavigne, Casimir, author.
Delpech, engineer.
Demidoff, Countess.
Denon, archæologist.
Desaugiers, poet.
De Sèze, defender of Louis XVI.
Domon, General.
Dorian, minister.
Duchesnois, actress.
Dupuytren, surgeon.
Duras, Duchess de.
Etienne, editor of the Constitutionnel.
February victims (1848.)
Feuchères, General.
Fould, minister of finance.

Foy, General.
Gaëte, Duke de, minister of finance.
Gay Lussac, chemist.
Genlis, Madame de, authoress.
Geoffroy St. Hilaire, naturalist.
Gobert, General.
Godoy, Spanish prince.
Gourgaud, General.
Gouvion St. Cyr, Marshal.
Grétry, composer.
Grouchy, Marshal.
Haxo, General of engineers.
Hérold, composer.
Jacotot, professor.
June victims (1848).
Junot, General.
Kellerman, Marshal.
Labédoyère, General.
Laffitte, banker.
La Fontaine, fabulist.
Laharpe, author.
Lalande, Admiral.
Laplace, astronomer.
Larrey, Baron, military physician.
Lauriston, Marshal.
Lavallette, Count de, minister.
Le Bas, engineer.
Lebrun, third consul.
Lecomte and Clément Thomas, Generals.
Ledru Rollin, organizer of universal suffrage in France.
Lefèbvre, Marshal.
Macdonald, Marshal.
Maison, Marshal.
Malet, General.
Manuel, orator.
Martignac, Viscount de, minister.
Masséna, Marshal.
Méhul, composer.
Michelet, historian.
Molière, dramatic author.
Monge, mathematician, member of Convention.
Morny, Duke de, minister.
Murat, King of Naples.

Murray, John, Generals.
Musset, Alfred de, poet.
Neigre, General.
Ney, Marshal.
Nodier, Charles, author.
Oude, Queen of.
Pacthod, General.
Pajol, General.
Parmentier, chemist.
Périer, Casimir, minister.
Pérignon, Marshal.
Poinsot, mathematician.
Poultier, member of Convention.
Pozzo di Borgo, Russian diplomatist.
Pradier, sculptor.
Rachel, actress.
Raguse, Duchess de.
Raspail, chemist.
Robertson, professor of physics.
Roederer, Count de, minister.
Rogniat, General.
Rossini, composer.
Rouget de l'Isle, composer of the "Marseillaise."
Savary, General.
Schickler, banker.
Scribe, dramatist.
Serrurier, Marshal.
Sieyès, abbé, second consul, 1799.
Soulié, Frédéric, author.
Soult, Marshal, Duke de Dalmatie.
Souvestre, Emile, novelist.
Suchet, Marshal.
Sydney Smith, Admiral Sir.
Talma, actor.
Thiers, President of Republic.
Valence, General.
Vallesteros, Spanish General.
Victims of the War of 1870-71.
Victor, Marshal.
Visconti, architect of the New Louvre.
Volney, philosopher.
Walewski, Count, minister.
Etc., etc., etc.

In visiting this interesting spot, it would be advisable to hire one of the guides at the entrance to point out the various tombs, as, of course, we cannot indicate them by mere description. The number of monuments, from the most magnificent mausoleum and obelisk down to the unpretending marble cross, amounts to upwards of 20,000. The walks are well shaded with plantations, and the elevated situation commands an admirable view of the interminable labyrinth of the city. It may here be observed, that it is the universal custom for persons encountering a funeral procession to remove their hats.

On May 28th, 1871, the insurgents of the Commune made this their last stronghold. They were at length surrounded by the victorious troops, and then commenced a scene of horror almost without parallel in the chequered annals of Paris. The insurgents were shot down to a man, and thus the last sparks of the insurrection extinguished.

Of all wars, a civil war is certainly the most cruel, the most unrelenting, and the most exterminating; and deep indeed must be the responsibility of those who, by their words or their actions, have contrived to set countryman against countryman, neighbour against neighbour, and very often brother against brother and father against child.

Place de la Bastille.

This Place, as its name indicates, was the site of the ancient Prison of State.

The Bastille was built in 1369 by Hugues Aubriot, Governor of Paris, and inventor of the first subterranean sewers. The name of this prison was long a terror to all classes of the French; and the deeds of violence and injustice which were perpetrated within its walls during four centuries will ever serve to keep in abomination the name of "king" in France. In the terrible Revolution of 1789, the incensed people attacked the Bastille with such irresistible force and determination that the garrison soon yielded, and in a short time all that remained of the old state prison was a heap of shapeless ruins. On the 10th of August, 1793, a fountain, called the Fountain of Regeneration, was erected upon the spot formerly occupied by the Bastille. This fountain represented Nature, and the water which spirted from her breasts was drunk by each of the eighty-six Commissioners of the first Assembly, who afterwards watered the ground in the vicinity, and christened it the Soil of Liberty. The fountain disappeared at the commencement of the First Empire, and it was replaced for a long time by the model of a colossal elephant, which was destroyed in 1834. In May, 1871, this was one of the last strongholds of the Communists, by whom every issue of the Place had been formidably barricaded, but it was captured, after a deadly struggle, by the Versailles troops on the 26th.

The fine column at present standing in the Place de la Bastille is called the *Colonne de Juillet*, and will be found described under this heading.

Place du Carrousel.

A large space between the Tuileries and the Louvre, which were united by the architect Visconti, during the reign of Napoleon III. The magnificent pile of buildings formed by the conjunction of these two palaces is perhaps unequalled in Europe.

Place du Château d'Eau.

In the centre of this large open space is a beautiful fountain, adorned with eight lions. On the northern side are seen two extensive piles of buildings—the first, a vast American circus, for the performance of equestrian feats; the second, a spacious barrack, capable of accommodating 8,000 men, connected with Vincennes and its military establishment by the long Boulevart Voltaire. The Place du Château d'Eau was the scene of a fearful struggle on May 25th, 1871. The insurgents occupied a strong position here, protected by barricades at every outlet. These were taken, one by one, by the Versailles troops, and the insurgents were driven back to the Bastille and Père La Chaise. All the neighbouring houses were completely riddled with balls and bullets, and a great many completely destroyed. The whole space is planted with trees, and a flower market is held here several times a week, especially on Mondays and Thursdays.

Place du Châtelet.

So called because here stood the prison of the Châtelet, a gloomy building whose walls had but too often echoed the groans of the victims of oppression, injustice, and intrigue: it was pulled down in 1802. In the centre of the Place is a fountain, the jets of water surrounding a column surmounted by a bronze statue representing Victory. On each side of the Place du Châtelet is a theatre—the Théâtre Historique, burned down in May, 1871, and now rebuilt; and the Théâtre du Châtelet, a part of which was also set fire to by the Commune.

Place de la Concorde.

The finest and most imposing square in Europe, and the culminating point of the splendour of Paris.

On the spot now occupied by the Obelisk, the guillotine was erected for the execution of Louis XVI. on January 21st, 1793. After a brief removal to the Place du Carrousel, the guillotine was again raised here, and more than 2,800 individuals were sacrificed to the bloodthirsty savages of 1793. Among those who terminated their career upon this awful spot were Charlotte Corday, the courageous patriot; Brissot, chief of the Girondins; Marie Antoinette, the beautiful queen; Philippe Egalité, Duke d'Orléans; Madame Roland, whose dying words were: "Oh Liberty! what crimes are committed in thy name!" Hébert; Danton; Camille Desmonlins; Chaumette; Madame Elisabeth, sister of Louis XVI.; Robespierre; St. Just; and hundreds of the French nobility.

Louis Philippe appropriated this spot to the erection of the *Obélisque de Lougsor*, which was brought from Egypt in 1832 by the architect Lebas, and was placed in its present situation in 1836. This obelisk ornamented the palace of the kings of Egypt at Thebes, about 1,500 years before the Christian era, and was a gift of Mehemet Ali, Pacha of Egypt, to the French government, at the same time that he gave a similar one to the English (the Cleopatra Needle). The expenses entailed by the transport to Paris and elevation of the obelisk in its present position amounted to two millions of francs, and, as the obelisk is 500,000 lbs. in weight, the stone of which it consists has cost four francs per pound! The pedestal on which it stands is a single block of grey granite from the quarries of Laber, in Brittany, weighing 240,000 lbs. Upon the northern side of this pedestal is represented the apparatus employed in the removal and embarkation of the beautiful Egyptian relic, and on the southern side that used in raising it in position. The obelisk itself is a magnificent monolith, a monument of solid, reddish granite, and is inscribed with three rows of deep, sharply cut, and well-preserved hieroglyphics on each side. On either side of this prodigious stone is a fountain executed in the best taste.

The eight statues placed round the Place de la Concorde represent the eight principal towns of France—Lyons, Marseilles, Bordeaux, Nantes, Rouen, Brest, Lille, and Strasburg.

In 1814 the Prussians and Russians, and in 1815 a part of the British army, were encamped on this Place. In March,

1871, the Prussians once more bivouacked in the Place de la Concorde and Champs Elysées, and in the following May it became the scene of a desperate struggle between the army of Versailles and the Communists.

Place du Trône.

In the centre of this large open space is a very fine fountain, and on each side two large and handsome classical columns surmounted by statues in bronze of Philippe Auguste and St. Louis. On a throne erected here Louis XIV. received the homage of his subjects in 1660, whence the present appellation of the Place. The guillotine stood here from June 9th to July 27th, 1794, during which time 1,270 persons were executed. Numerous boulevarts and avenues diverge hence in every direction. A gingerbread fair is held here annually.

Place des Victoires.

In 1684, François d'Aubusson, Duke de la Feuillade, loaded with goods and honours by his king, Louis XIV., wished to open this place to the honour of his sovereign. He purchased the ground for 500,000 *livres*, and spent a still greater sum on the monument. In 1686, a statue of Louis XIV. was erected in gilt bronze on a pedestal of marble, twenty-two feet in height. During the great Revolution, this statue was demolished, and a pyramid erected on its site, upon which was inscribed a list of victorious battles fought by the republican armies. Hence the name of the Place des Victoires. In 1806, Napoleon I. caused a colossal bronze statue to be erected to General Desaix, who was represented naked; the bad taste and indecency of this work caused its removal in 1814. At the Restoration, Louis XVIII. once more placed on its former site an equestrian statue of Louis XIV., and it remains to this day. This splendid statue was designed by Bosio, and weighs 16,000 lbs. The figure of the horse, in a rearing attitude, rests on the hind-legs and tail; the rider is garbed as a Roman general. The long inscriptions record that the statue was erected to replace the original one; and the *reliefs* at the sides represent the passage of the Rhine by Louis XIV. in 1672, and the monarch distributing military honours.

Pont Neuf.

Is the longest and the most frequented bridge in Paris, and answers to our London Bridge. It is a popular saying that a

priest, a white horse, and a soldier are always to be seen here.
Our readers will have the opportunity of testing the truth of the
saying. This bridge is divided in two by the point of the
island of La Cité, and in the centre stands a bronze statue of
Henry IV., by Lemot. The height of this beautiful statue is 14
feet, and its weight 30,000 lbs. The pedestal, of white marble,
is approached by seven steps of the same, running all round, and
bears a Latin inscription commemorating the inauguration in
1818. At the sides are two *bas reliefs* in bronze: Henry IV.
causing bread to be distributed among the citizens of Paris, who
had sought protection of him during the siege, and his halt at
Notre Dame, where he causes peace to be proclaimed to the
inhabitants by the provost of Paris.

Porte St. Denis.

Built in 1672 by the city of Paris to celebrate the conquests
of Louis XIV., and then forming one of the gates of the city,
the walls of which ran along the present Boulevarts. It is about
80 feet high, and of more symmetrical proportions than the adjoining Porte St. Martin. The archway is 46 feet in height and
26 feet in width. The Latin inscription on the southern side is
to the following effect: *To Louis the Great, for having within
sixty days crossed the Rhine, the Waal, the Meuse, and the Issel,
conquered three provinces, and captured forty fortified cities*. The
two groups of statuary at the base of the pyramids are all allegorical figures—one representing vanquished Holland in the character of a terrified woman, seated upon a dying lion, who holds
in his paws seven arrows representing the seven United Provinces; the other the Rhine, holding a horn of plenty. In July,
1830, the insurgents occupied the top of this arch, and defied all
the efforts of the troops to dislodge them. The sanguinary revolt
of 1848 began in this quarter. A barricade of the Communists
erected here was only captured by the Versailles troops after
several fierce attacks and great loss of life to either side.

Porte St. Martin.

A triumphal arch, in close proximity to the Porte St. Denis,
constructed in 1674 in honour of Louis XIV. The inscriptions
and *reliefs* commemorate the victories of that monarch. On the
southern side are represented the capture of Besançon and the
defeat of the Germans, Spaniards, and Dutch, and on the
northern side the taking of Limbourg and the victory over the
Germans. On the 31st March, 1814, the German and Russian

armies entered Paris by the Faubourg St. Martin, and passed
through the Porte St. Martin and the Boulevarts to the Place de
la Concorde. The insurgents in 1830 established themselves on
the top of this monument also, and defied for some time the efforts
of the soldiers. Many a bloody encounter took place here in
June 1848. One of the most formidable barricades of the Communists was constructed here across the Boulevart, which it
completely commanded. This neighbourhood was the scene of
another of the most brutal excesses of the Commune, the insurgents entering the house of a *restaurateur* in close proximity to
the Porte St. Martin, and after taking possession of the cellar and
its contents, proceeding to occupy the house with the view of
firing on the troops from the windows. The terrified inmates
entreated them to desist from their purpose, and even struck one
of the intruders. This formed the signal for a general massacre,
and the insurgents, maddened by defeat, rage, and despair, pursued
and pitilessly murdered every man, woman, and child whom they
found in the building, about fifty in all. They then proceeded
to set fire to the premises, which, together with the adjoining
houses and the theatre of the Porte St. Martin, were soon
reduced to one heap of black and smouldering ruins.

Prison Mazas.

A gloomy edifice, opposite the Lyons Railway Station, constructed on the well-known cellular system. This prison is
reserved for persons awaiting trial, and contains 1,260 cells.
Its annual cost to the city is about £40,000.

Prison de la Roquette.

The Newgate of Paris, where criminals of the most desperate
character are confined previous to their execution or conveyance
to the galleys. Just opposite to the gate of this prison is the
public place of execution by the guillotine. An excellent
description of this prison and the condemned cell is to be found
in Victor Hugo's " Dernier Jour d'un Condamné." The
Prison de la Roquette was the scene of one of the most melancholy tragedies enacted during the Commune. On May 24th,
Archbishop Darboy and five priests, imprisoned as hostages,
were conducted to the outer courtyard of the prison, where they
were brutally shot by order of one of the leaders of the Commune, and their bodies thrown into a hole at Père La Chaise.
On the 26th, thirty-seven other prisoners were murdered in cold

blood; and on the 27th, seventy *gendarmes* were indiscriminately slaughtered by the mob of condemned convicts released for the purpose of acting as executioners. The approach of the troops, who were now masters of the entire city, fortunately soon compelled the murderers to retreat, otherwise all the surviving hostages of the Commune would infallibly have shared the same appalling fate as the gendarmes.

Puits Artésien.

An artesian well, situated in the centre of the Place de Breteuil, near the Ecole Militaire, interesting even to the non-professional visitor. The well, over which rises an open-work iron tower 128 feet in height, is 1,900 feet in depth, and yields upwards of 200,000 gallons of water daily. This, with three new artesian wells, forms one of the chief sources for the supply of the extensive waterworks of Paris. In winter, when the temperature is low, the well emits volumes of vapour.

St. Ambroise.

A fine new church, in the Boulevart Voltaire, replacing another, which was of some historical interest. In 1790, this church was devoted to the Goddess of Reason, whilst a revolutionary committee sat in the porter's lodge. The cellars were also utilized, being converted into a common "tap."

St. Augustin.

This handsome church, of a particularly bold style of architecture, is situated at the intersection of the Boulevarts Haussmann and Malesherbes, and was completed in 1868 by the architect Baltard. It is surmounted by four octagonal towers flanking a huge central cupola. In front are three entrances, above which rises a large circular window crowned with a gable.

St. Etienne du Mont.

A church behind the Panthéon. One of the oldest of Paris, the first stone having been laid, it is said, in 1121. The curious square tower, flanked at one of its angles by a lofty circular turret, dates from the twelfth century. The principal *façade*, which was erected in 1610 by Marguerite de Valois, is rather singular in aspect, being a most curious mixture of different architectural styles. The interior is extremely interesting, and some very fine paintings deserve the attention of the visitor. The tombs of Ste. Geneviève, the patroness saint of Paris, Pascal, the great philosopher, and Racine, the celebrated poet, are in this church, which, from the rich effect produced by its peculiar construction, its frescoes, and its other ornaments, is one of the most interesting of the capital. At the grand altar of this church, the Archbishop of Paris, Sibour, was assassinated by Verger, a half-mad priest, in 1857.

St. Eustache.

St. Eustache, a church directly facing the Halles Centrales, is a building that cannot fail to strike the eye, not on account of its architectural beauties, but from something solid and massive in its appearance, standing, as it does, in the midst of the busy crowds that throng the market. The first stone of this church was laid in 1532, but it was not finished till 1642, thus occupying 110 years in its construction. The style of architecture is a strange mixture of degenerate Gothic and modern art, and is not in the very best taste. The proportions of the interior are graceful and lofty, and produce a good general effect. The choir was struck by several projectiles during the bombardment of 1870-71, and seriously injured. Part of the edifice near the clock caught fire on one of these occasions, but the flames were speedily extinguished. St. Eustache is one of the most frequented churches in Paris, especially on festivals, on account of the superior music.

St. Germain l'Auxerrois.

The origin of this church, situated opposite the Louvre, is uncertain. It was pillaged and destroyed by the Normans, and rebuilt by King Robert, in the eleventh century. The remarkable lowness of the roof gives it a depressed character. There is a sinister interest attached to this church, on account of its bell having given the signal for the fearful massacre of St. Bartholomew, in 1572. During the whole of that night of horror this bell unremittingly tolled its funeral peal. The Protestant can scarcely look upon this building without emotion. History tells us that it was from one of the windows of the Louvre, facing the river, that the infamous Charles IX. fired upon the 100,000 doomed opponents of the Church of Rome.

> "Then babe and mother shriek'd in vain for aid—
> Then sire and son fell headlong in their gore
> The fierce fanatic's vengeful, hateful blade
> Uplifted fell, and mercy knew no more."

During the Revolution of 1789, the edifice escaped with little damage. On the 13th of February, 1831, an attempt having been made to celebrate in it the anniversary of the murder of the Duke de Berri, a tumult arose, and everything within the church was destroyed. It was then shut up till 1837, when it was repaired, and again restored to public worship. The entire decoration of the interior is, therefore, of very recent origin.

St. Germain des Prés.

At the junction of the Rue Bonaparte and the Rue de Rennes is situated St. Germain des Prés, the oldest church in Paris. It was erected in 990; but the lower walls of the large square tower at the western end are supposed to be of the sixth century. In 1369 the church was fortified against the English by Charles V., and in the time of Henry IV. it still resembled a fortress. In the Prison de l'Abbaye, which stood behind, took place the revolting massacre of September 2, 1792.

St. Gervais.

Behind the Hôtel de Ville is situated the Gothic church of St. Gervais, finished in 1420, except the Classical front, which was added in 1616. This church is not devoid of merit, and produces a very handsome effect.

St. Jacques du Haut Pas.

The Church of St. Jacques du Haut Pas is situated in the Rue St. Jacques, between the Val de Grâce and the Panthéon. It was finished in 1684, and its style is Doric. The interior is decorated with numerous paintings.

St. Laurent.

A very fine church, built in 1429, with a recently added front. The ogive is painted, and illustrates the life and death of St. Lawrence. It is situated in the immediate vicinity of the Strasbourg Railway Station.

St. Paul.

This fine church is in the Rue St. Antoine, and was begun in 1627. Cardinal Richelieu performed mass in it in 1641.

The church is cruciform, and its dome was the first built in Paris. Many celebrities were buried here, but the Great Revolution swept away their tombs. Here, also, were deposited the hearts of Louis XIII. and Louis XIV. And not far from them was buried *l'homme au masque de fer*, the mysterious captive of Louis XIV.

St. Roch.

In the Rue St. Honoré. One of the most fashionable churches in Paris, but also one of the ugliest, and interesting only as showing the transition from the style of Louis XIV. to that of Louis XV. Pierre Corneille and Descartes are buried here. It was opposite to this church that, in 1795, General Bonaparte fired upon the royalists who were advancing against the Directory, and thus checked the progress of the counter-revolution.

St. Sulpice.

This is the most important and the richest church on the left bank of the Seine. Its proportions are strikingly grand. It was commenced in 1646, but not completed until a century later. The form of the church is a cross, 460 feet in length, and 185 feet in breadth. The front, consisting of a portico supported by fluted Doric columns below, surmounted by Ionic columns above, is crowned by two towers, the highest of which is 231 feet from the ground. At the entrance are placed, as receptacles for holy water, two remarkably large shells, which rest upon curious rockwork of marble, executed by Pigalle; they were presented to Francis I. by the Republic of Venice. The principal objects of interest in the interior are: the frescoes in the chapels; the old stained glass of great merit which adorns the windows; the statues of the Virgin, of St. Paul, and St. John; the high altar, splendidly decorated with gilt ornaments; and the pulpit, adorned with figures of Faith, Hope, and Charity. The organ is richly carved, and is externally the finest in Paris. On the floor is a meridian line terminated by a white marble obelisk in the northern transept.

St. Vincent de Paul.

Situated in the Rue de Lafayette, in the vicinity of the Northern Railway Station. A large and gorgeous modern church, with two square towers in the façade, and nearly on the model of the early Christian Basilicas at Rome. It is finely situated on an elevation, with steps and slopes leading up to it. It was completed in 1844 at an expense of £248,000.

Ste. Chapelle.

Rises in the southern court of the Palais de Justice, and is one of the best specimens of the art of the Middle Ages. It was erected in 1242, by the architect Pierre de Montereau, to receive the supposed fragments of the crown of thorns, the true cross, and the garment of the Saviour, as well as the head of the spear with which his side was pierced, which are said to have been purchased by St. Louis from Jean de Brienne, King of Jerusalem, and his son-in-law Baldwin, Emperor of Byzantium, for the sum of two million francs. The chapel, a perfect gem of its kind, and the most beautiful Gothic edifice in Paris, fortunately escaped destruction in 1871, although almost entirely surrounded by a blazing mass of buildings. The height is about 150 feet, length 130 feet, and breadth 42 feet. The truly elegant gilt spire distinguishes this chapel at a great distance.

Ste. Clotilde.

Is situated near the Palais Bourbon, and is one of the newest churches in Paris. It is of the Gothic style, and its towers are conspicuous objects. The cost of the building amounted to 8,000,000 francs.

Sorbonne.

This edifice, situated Place de la Sorbonne, is divided into two sections: the Church of the Sorbonne and the buildings of the Univerity of Paris.

The University, which many theological disputes has rendered famous, as it not unfrequently even opposed the authority of the Popes, owes its name to its founder, Robert Sorbonne, the confessor of Louis XI., and was erected in 1250. In 1808, the Sorbonne became the seat of the Academy of Paris, and now contains a library of 80,000 volumes and a good museum of natural history, etc. This building is often mentioned by the various French authors, and, indeed, at one time it enjoyed an immense celebrity on account of the violence with which the religious arguments were carried on. Many eminent men have filled the Professor's chair at the Sorbonne; and among others may be mentioned MM. Villemain, Victor Cousin, Guizot, etc.

The Church, Palladian in style, and simple, is a pleasing composition, the first stone of which was laid by the celebrated Cardinal Duke de Richelieu, in 1629. The interior is cruciform, and in a recess on the right is the tomb of the Cardinal, a *chef d'œuvre* of Girardon, executed in 1694, and one of the finest pieces of sculpture of the seventeenth century; on it is the statue of the cardinal, sustained by Religion. During the Revolution of 1789, this tomb was desecrated, and the head of Cardinal Richelieu paraded through the streets on a pike. It was only reunited to the body in 1866, after a separation of seventy-seven years.

Statue of Marshal Ney.

Stands near the Luxembourg Gardens, and marks the precise spot where Marshal Ney, *le brave des braves*, was shot. This brave but misguided man was, at his own desire, sent by Louis XVIII. to repulse Napoleon after the landing from Elba; but, instead of doing so, he packed up his old uniform in his portmanteau, and went over with his army to the Emperor. For this he was subsequently sentenced to death by the Chamber of Peers, and shot, the very next day, where his statue now stands. This statue, cast in bronze from a design by Rude, represents the dauntless general in a commanding attitude, animating his followers to advance.

Tour St. Jacques

At the corner of the Place du Châtelet, facing the Rue de Rivoli, stands the Tour St. Jacques La Boucherie, a handsome square Gothic tower, 187 feet in height, now the sole remnant of a church which was destroyed during the Revolution, in 1789. This interesting structure dates from the time of Francis I., and occupies the centre of a small public garden, where great numbers of the victims of the Revolution of 1871 were interred. The tower has always been considered one of the exquisite specimens of its style. The statue in the centre is that of Pascal, the philosopher. The view from the summit well repays the trouble of mounting 294 steps. A small fee is paid at the entrance.

Tribunal de Commerce.

A fine new edifice at the corner of the Quai de la Cité and the Boulevart du Palais, the first of the commercial courts of law, completed in 1866. This building, which has cost upwards of £200,000 sterling, is one of the finest and chastest of the modern edifices of Paris. The courts are open to the public, and sit daily, the judges being commercial men, appointed by the commercial body of the city. The whole of this part of old Paris was granted by Dagobert to his goldsmith and minister, St. Eloi, and called "La Ceinture de St. Eloi." St. Marcel was buried in one of the streets which intersected this ground. The legends connected with this quarter of Paris are innumerable.

Trinité (La).

A church opposite the Rue de la Chaussée d'Antin. Is a splendid specimen of the late Renaissance style, completed in 1866 at a cost of 11,000,000 francs. A delightful public garden lies in front of it.

Tuileries.

The Palace of the Tuileries was originally built by Catherine de Médicis, in 1564, in order to have a separate residence from that of her son Charles IX., who then remained at the Louvre. It occupies the site of a former brick or tile-yard, whence its appellation. The celebrated Philibert Delorme was the architect, and it was enlarged under Henry IV., Louis XIII., and Louis XIV.

No edifice in Paris is so rich in historical associations as the Tuileries, and none, with the single exception of the Hôtel de Ville, has ever been overtaken by so terrible a fate. On August 10th, 1792, after a fierce contest, the palace was taken by storm by an infuriated populace, and its defenders, consisting of a number of French nobles, 1000 Swiss guards and 26 officers, 100 domestics of the palace, and 200 national guards, mercilessly butchered. On July 29th, 1830, the Tuileries was again captured, and the furniture plundered or destroyed. But Louis Philippe reinstated it in great splendour, and was in it when the Revolution of 1848 took place. Although there were abundance of troops to defend the palace, he preferred leaving it, and made his escape through the gardens. The capture of the palace was succeeded by the most frightful scenes of devastation. The royal carriages and furniture were burned in the courtyard, and the throne was carried to the Place de la Bastille and burnt also.

On May 20th, 1871, the Communists, aware of their desperate position and impending destruction, determined at one of their secret meetings to wreak their revenge on the ill-fated city by setting all the principal public buildings on fire. The prelude to the appalling scene which ensued consisted in placing combustibles soaked with petroleum, and barrels of gunpowder in the buildings doomed to destruction. The Tuileries was one of the first edifices subjected to this fearfully comprehensive and diabolical scheme. It was set on fire in a number of different places on the 22nd May, the day after the Versailles troops had obtained an entrance into the city, but before they had gained possession of the palace. The conflagration soon assumed the most terrible dimensions, and all attempts to extinguish it were entirely fruitless. The whole of the western side of the palace facing the Jardin des Tuileries, and the pavilion on the north side next to the Rue de Rivoli, were reduced to a gigantic heap of smouldering ruins, after burning three days and nights.*

Val de Grâce.

A large military hospital, situated Rue St. Jacques. This building was converted into an hospital by Napoleon I., it having been originally a Benedictine nunnery, founded in 1642 by Anne of Austria in gratitude for the birth of a son (Louis XIV.) The edifice was struck by 150 shells during the siege, and its medical staff only escaped being shot by the Communists by the timely arrival of the Versailles troops. In the great court is a bronze statue of the celebrated surgeon Larrey, by David d'Angers; on the pedestal of white marble are four *bas reliefs* of the battles of the Beresina, the Pyramids,

---

* At the time of going to press an order has been signed for rasing the ruins of the palace of the Tuileries. It is always with regret that the disappearance of historical monuments is seen; but, in a modern city, if a ruin cannot be repaired it must be cleared away. The northern wing of the new Louvre is now rapidly approaching completion, and, as soon as the ruins of the Tuileries are removed, and the space between the gardens and the Place du Carrousel arranged, either in garden or otherwise, the imposing mass of buildings forming the Old and New Louvre will be in a fit state to present itself to the admiring gaze of the tourist.

Austerlitz, and Sommo Sierra, at which he distinguished himself. But the chief object of historical interest is the Church in front of the principal court. This edifice is remarkable for its dome, an object very conspicuous from every part of Paris. The first stone was laid by Louis XIII. in 1645.

In 1675, Mademoiselle de la Vallière and Madame de Montespan, the discarded mistresses of Louis XIV., retired to the Val de Grâce previous to their taking the veil.

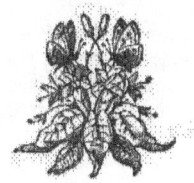

Environs of Paris.

Asnières.

A pretty village, nearly every house of which is a small villa, and which was pillaged and severely injured during the two sieges of 1870-71. The park of Asnières is a place of public amusement, and is much frequented in the summer season for the concerts, balls, and fireworks which are held there. Pleasure-boats on hire.

Bourget (Le).

This village was the scene of several very fierce engagements during the siege; first taken by 600 *Francs Tireurs de la Presse* on October 28, 1870, it was attacked by 24,000 Prussians on the following day, and, after a severe bombardment, retaken by them on the 30th. Nearly all the *Francs Tireurs* were slain.

Buzenval.

An important position which the French conquered in their last great sortie of January 19th, 1871. The battle of Buzenval, though bloody and honourable, was hopeless, Paris being already at that date on the verge of famine.

Champigny.

On November 29th, 1870, all was ready for the great battle. The next day, the whole of the French army, 100,000 strong, crossed the Marne at Joinville, under cover of the guns of the forts. The French made rapid progress; the Prussians were forced from their lines; and the village of Champigny was carried after a deadly struggle. As the sun went down, the cannonade gradually died away, and the cold became most intense. There was a cessation of hostilities on December 1st, for the purpose of relieving the wounded and burying the dead. But on the 2nd, the terrible roar and thunder again reverberated through the battlefield, and throughout its beautiful but deserted environs. The weather was fine and clear, and the landscape comprised a vast extent of hill and valley and river. The Marne describes a horseshoe behind Champigny, Villiers, and Brie. The Prussians attacked these positions at daybreak, and although the French were well supplied with powerful artillery, thundering forth from three forts and several redoubts, thousands upon thousands of them turned and tumbled back in appalling confusion to the very banks of the river, and 400 pieces of cannon came tumbling after them. A river is said to be a great disadvantage to an army; in this instance it brought the fugitives to a stand and to their senses. A general, who was near when the panic began, rode up to the soldiers with such resolution of language and seriousness of front, that his presence was at once a reproach and an inspiration. He said little, but did much, and what he said was said calmly. He cried: "Follow me, my men, where duty as well as danger calls; let us save France, whatever becomes of us." The troops rallied, and followed, and fought most desperately. The Prussians were again driven from all their positions, and from more than the ground they occupied the day before; and at night it was a grand sight to see the whole French army camping on the conquered field of battle. Another dreadful frost having set in, the commander-in-chief gave the order for all the troops to retreat on the 3rd. The estimated losses on both sides were the following: French, 6,000; Prussians, 20,000. A monument erected on the plateau of Champigny commemorates the event.

Compiègne.

Is pleasantly situated on the river Oise, and has always been a favourite residence of the monarchs of France. It is well worth a visit. Near the bridge is an ancient, dilapidated tower, where, on May 25th, 1430, Joan of Arc, the Maid of Orleans, was taken prisoner by the English. She had conducted a sally from the tower, but as she was about to re-enter it, the portcullis was dropped by the commandant, who was jealous of her reputation, and she was thus betrayed to her enemies. Compiègne is an agreeable summer residence, and attracts numerous visitors.

Enghien.

A small watering-place possessing a sulphureous spring. There is a lake, with boats; and many pleasant walks and drives in the vicinity. It is a favourite holiday resort of the Parisians.

Fontainebleau.

Those who desire to visit Fontainebleau should devote an entire day to the excursion, and leave Paris by an early train, reaching their destination in one hour and a half. One hour will probably suffice for the inspection of the palace and garden, after which a drive or walk to the *Gorges de Franchard* will occupy two or three hours, and a visit to the *Fort de l'Empereur* one hour. If the stranger purposes dining at Fontainebleau, he will do well on his arrival to order a dinner at an hotel for the hour at which he intends to return from his walk. To visit the scenery of the forest completely, vehicles are always in readiness, but the price must be bargained for beforehand. A Sunday pleasure train runs during the summer at reduced fares.

Joinville Le Pont.

A pretty village, commanding picturesque views of the windings of the river Marne. Pleasure-boats can be hired here for excursions in the vicinity, which abounds in fine scenery. Near Joinville is the Canal St. Maur, a very curious tunnel, 1,800 feet in length by 30 in width and height, cut through the solid rock for shortening the navigation of the Marne.

Mont Valérien.

A calvary in former times stood on this hill, and was the popular resort of devotees until 1830. In 1841 it was converted into one of the strongest forts connected with the defence of Paris. In 1870-71 the fort played a prominent part in the siege. On March 18th, 1871, when the insurgents on Montmartre had defied the attempt of General Vinoy to take from them the 250 cannons which they had seized, M. Thiers ordered all the forts to be evacuated by the Versailles army, including Mont Valérien, the citadel of Paris. This order was being carried out, when General Vinoy insisted on its re-occupation. This was hardly done, when a Communist force reached the gates to take possession. A few days later, the guns of Mont

Valérien raked the column of insurgents marching confidently under its walls, on its way to capture Versailles and the Government of M. Thiers, cutting the column in two, and contributing mainly to the failure of that enterprise. The view from the summit is delightful.

St. Cloud.

Was originally the country seat of Francis I. The palace was increased under the reign of Louis XIV. to a considerable extent. In 1589, Henry III. was stabbed here by Jacques Clément, a fanatical monk of the order of Dominicans. In 1799, Napoleon Bonaparte dispersed the Council of Five Hundred, and then caused himself to be nominated First Consul. To these reminiscences of the first rise of his power is ascribed the marked preference of Napoleon I. for St. Cloud. The palace was chosen as head-quarters of the Allies in 1815, and the capitulation of Paris was signed here. Here also, in 1830, Charles X. signed the decrees for the abolition of the freedom of the press, dissolution of the Chambers, etc., which led to his downfall. St. Cloud afterwards became the principal summer residence of Napoleon III., and afforded hospitality to Queen Victoria in 1855. The palace was destroyed in 1870 by shells from Mont Valérien, in order to dislodge the Germans sheltered within, and is now a mere shell. As for the town itself, it was utterly destroyed in 1871, the Prussians having set fire to it with the aid of petroleum, several days after the armistice had been concluded! The church, of a Romanesque style of architecture, was the only edifice which escaped unharmed. No town in the environs of Paris suffered so severely as St. Cloud, or presented so melancholy an appearance after the termination of the war. The park, laid out by the celebrated Le Nôtre, and considered his masterpiece, contains some very fine walks and avenues, statues, pieces of water, cascades, shady glades, etc. There are many points commanding lovely prospects, the best being from the site of the *Lanterne de Diogene*, a tower built by Napoleon I., but destroyed by the Prussians during the autumn of 1870. The eye takes in hence admirable glimpses of the surrounding scenery: a large part of Paris, the windings of the Seine, and many other picturesque views too numerous to mention. Owing to the railroad, tramways, and steamers, St. Cloud attracts vast crowds, especially on Sundays. All the ground adjoining St.

Cloud possesses historical interest in connection with the great siege of 1870.

St. Denis.

The sole object of a visit to St. Denis will be the celebrated Abbey Church, where thirty-five kings and nineteen queens of France have been interred. St. Denis was occupied by the French throughout the entire period of the first siege, toward the close of which the Prussians resolved to dislodge them. During the last three days before the capitulation of Paris, they accordingly bombarded the town with unremitting violence. Many houses were destroyed on this occasion, and the abbey church sustained severe injury. The town was occupied by the Prussians after the capitulation, and was finally evacuated by them in September, 1871. From the summit of the church a splendid panorama, measuring upwards of 200 kilomètres in circuit, will be enjoyed. Amongst other places which are observable from this eminence may be mentioned Bondy, Aubervilliers, La Courneuve, Drancy, Le Bourget, Le Blanc Mesnil, Pont Iblon, Dugny, Gonesse, Stains, Pierrefitte, Villetaneuse, Montmorency, Epinay, Argenteuil, Colombes, the plain of Gennevilliers, St. Ouen, St. Germain, the citadel of Mont Valérien, etc., etc.

St. Germain.

A quiet town, indebted for its foundation to the palace, a large gloomy edifice, constructed principally of brick, in the vicinity of the railway station; it was the favourite residence of Francis I., Henry II., Henry IV., and the birthplace of Henry II., Charles IX., and Louis XIV. The principal charm of St. Germain consists in the terrace, which extends for upwards of two miles along the eastern slope of the hill at a considerable elevation above the Seine, and commands a fine view of the valley, the winding river, and the well-peopled plain. At the base of the hill are situated the villages of Le Pecq and Le Vésinet, to the right Marly, its aqueduct, and Louveciennes, and in the distance the towers of St. Denis. Paris itself is concealed from view by the Mont Valérien. The beautiful and extensive forest of St. Germain is preserved in admirable order, and affords abundant shade and retirement. The elevated and salubrious situation of this small town renders it a favourite summer residence of the Parisians, as well as of a number of English families. M. Thiers died here, September 3, 1877.

Sèvres.

Known to have existed in 560. Is prettily situated on the river Seine, where the hills close on each side. Its porcelain manufactory, of world-wide fame, is supported by Government at considerable expense. The first house on the left, across the bridge, is the one where Prince Bismarck and M. Jules Favre held their interview for the signature of the armistice, in 1871.

Versailles.

Were Paris blotted from the face of the earth, leaving nothing behind it but the Palace of Versailles, the journey to this fairy-like structure would alone well repay the visitor.

The town, of 65,000 inhabitants, has little to attract the stranger beyond the Church of Notre Dame; the Place Hoche, in which stands a fine bronze statue of that general; the Cathedral of St. Louis; and the Jeu de Paume, memorable in history as the spot where, in 1789, a nobleman, appearing as the king's deputy and pronouncing the National Assembly sitting there dissolved, received the audacious reply from Mirabeau, " Allez dire à votre maître que nous sommes ici par la volonté du peuple, et que nous n'en sortirons que par la force des bayonnettes." The Palace and Park of Versailles, termed by Voltaire *l'abîme des dépenses*, are so extensive that it is indispensable to hire a guide in order to thoroughly explore them. In front of the palace is the Cour d'Honneur, separated from the Place d'Armes by stone parapets, flanking a heavy iron railing richly ornamented with gilt. At the extremities of this railing are groups representing (on the right) France victorious over Austria, (on the left) France victorious over Spain. In the court are placed two rows of colossal statues; (to the right) Richelieu, Bayard, Colbert, Marshal Jourdan, Marshal Massena, Admiral Tourville, Admiral Duguay Trouin, and Turenne; (to the left) Suger, Duguesclin, Sully, Marshal Lannes, Marshal Mortier, Admiral Suffren, Admiral Duquesne, and Condé. At the upper part of the court stands a colossal equestrian statue of Louis XIV., made of cannon brought from the Rhine. The rich museum, unparalleled in Europe, was founded by Louis Philippe in 1832. It is replete with historical paintings, and the mass is so overwhelming that a walk through all the galleries without a single halt will alone occupy an hour and a-half. As historical illustration was always predominant, works were received without regard to their merits as works of art. The critical eye, therefore, will not fail to detect inferior productions intermingled with the efforts of transcendent genius. In the Park and Gardens, laid out by the eminent Le Nôtre, are trees several centuries old, numerous large and magnificent fountains, groups most elaborately sculptured, a vast number of marble statues and vases—some of the former copies from celebrated antiques, others originals of the seventeenth century. About a mile from the terrace of the palace are situated the Trianons, two fine mansions, in the largest of which took place the trial of Marshal Bazaine, and near to which are kept the celebrated State Carriages.

The Palace of Versailles was originally a small *château*, of red brick, erected by Louis XIII. In 1660, Louis XIV. conceived the idea of enlarging his predecessor's castle and converting it into the magnificent royal residence we now see; this stupendous undertaking was completed in 1681 by the architect Mansard. The king died here in 1715. Here took place the birth and death of Louis XV. And here, too, Damiens made his attempt to assassinate this monarch in 1757. Louis XVI. resided here until 1789, when he was removed by force to Paris. In 1795 the palace became a manufactory of arms, and supplied the French army annually with 50,000 muskets. In 1815 it was pillaged by the Prussians. Louis XVIII., Charles X., and Louis Philippe occupied it; and in 1855 it was used by Napoleon III. for the reception of Her Majesty Queen Victoria. From September, 1870, to March, 1871, the palace of Versailles was the headquarters of the Prussians; and a great part of the edifice was employed as a military hospital, the pictures being carefully covered to protect them from injury. In the Cour d'Honneur King William of Prussia was proclaimed Emperor of Germany in the midst of his victorious generals and army, January 18th, 1871. To describe minutely all the events which occurred at Versailles during the above period would be to write an entire history of the Franco-Prussian war—a task far beyond the scope of this Handbook. Suffice it to say that this town, usually so dull and peaceful, then formed the great centre of operations of the most remarkable war ever witnessed in the world's history, whilst a little later, when Paris was seized by the Commune, it became the seat of the new French Republican Government. At this present moment a portion of the

Palace of Versailles is the seat of the Senate and Chamber of Deputies.

The Museum is visible every day but Monday. The *Grandes Eaux*, or Waterworks, play in the Gardens once a month in summer, and are advertised about a week beforehand. This exhibition is computed to cost over £400 on each occasion, and the sight is almost worth the trouble of crossing the Atlantic to witness.

Ville d'Avray.

A Prussian battery was established here during the great siege of 1870-71. The spot is very beautiful, and contains a small cemetery, where the Prussian officers are buried.

Vincennes.

A commune of over 17,000 inhabitants, situated five miles to the east of Paris, and celebrated for its castle, donjon, gatehouse, chapel, fortress, fort, ancient forest, polygon, etc. The platform of the donjon, a massive square stone tower, with four smaller towers at its angles, commands a splendid view over the adjacent country. The walls of this structure are of prodigious strength, being seventeen feet thick. The ceilings are vaulted and groined, and the double doors sheathed with thick iron. The whole aspect of the tower is singularly gloomy. The torture-room, as employed in the twelfth century, is still to be seen on the ground-floor. A volume might be filled with the names of all the prisoners confined here under *lettres de cachet*. The list includes :—Enguerrand de Marigny (1315); Henry IV. (1574); Prince de Condé (1617); Marshal d'Ornano and Marie de Gonzague (1626); Duke de Beaufort (1643); Princes de Condé and de Conti, and Duke de Longueville (1650); Cardinal de Retz (1652); Nicolas Fouquet (1661); Marquises de Châtillon, de Clermont, and de Polignac (1717); Prince Edward (1748); Count de Mirabeau (1777); Duke d'Engbien, previous to being shot in the ditch of the fortress (1804); Bishops of Gand, Tournay, and Troyes (1811); the ministers of Charles X. (1830); the conspirators of May and the insurgents of June (1848); and many members of the National Assembly (1851). The castle, or château, was founded by Louis Le Jeune in 1137, and subsequently became a royal residence. The last monarch who resided here was Louis XV. The fortress was alternately captured by the

English and the French during the wars of the fifteenth century. The chapel was begun in 1248 and finished in 1552. The gatehouse, called "Tour Principale," is a large rectangular tower, 115 feet high, protected by a moat and a loop-holed wall in front. The new fort was constructed by Louis Philippe in 1849, and contains immense barracks, stabling for 1250 horses, two powder-magazines, and an immense park of artillery. The beautiful and extensive forest and park contain many lovely drives and walks, pieces of water, shady glades, etc. St. Louis frequently administered justice under an oak here, at a spot marked by a stone pyramid. The polygon is a space where mounds of earth are erected as targets for gun and rifle practice, as at Wimbledon; it is connected with an extensive military exercising-ground, known as the esplanade.

In May, 1871, Vincennes was one of the last places occupied by the Communists, but they were compelled to evacuate it on the approach of the Versailles army, leaving one of their number concealed in a casemate of the fort with instructions to set fire to the powder-magazine when the troops had entered. This unfortunate wretch, whom certain death awaited in any case, preferred suicide to the execution of his terrible commission. On this occasion, four hundred insurgents, unable to effect their retreat, surrendered *à discrétion*. They were, nevertheless, doomed to be butchered by the exasperated soldiers, who had sworn to show no mercy: there was one tremendous volley, and all was over.

Paris Universal Exhibition, 1878.

We have long passed the period when it was necessary to discuss the value of Exhibitions in order to secure for them the attention they deserve. Thanks to the rapidity of communication, to the removal of barriers with which nations formerly surrounded themselves, to the commercial liberties which are becoming acclimatized everywhere, and to the acts both of governments and peoples, hostilities are dying out, old rivalries are changing into honourable emulation, prohibitions are disappearing, nations respect each other in proportion as they are better acquainted, and we may look forward to a not distant period, when all humanity shall be united by peace in one great family, the members of which will in future only use their hands to combat the fury of the elements, and only employ the grand forces of nature in contributing to the welfare of all the world.

As the horizon expands every day before the human mind, how vast is the growth of the field cultivated by intelligence! What gigantic works remain to be done by us, and by those who come after us! And yet what grand, what noble things have already been done! Exhibitions tell all this to those who will hear and see. They are inventories, in relief, of works accomplished and knowledge acquired, just as encyclopædias are the written ones. In proportion as works accumulate, exhibitions become so much the more necessary; they are more sought after, more frequented, and more appreciated. But yesterday the whole world was invited to admire that marvellous temple where the God of Labour spread out his choicest productions in infinite variety. To-day, but on a grander scale, the Exhibition of Paris recalls that of Philadelphia, both by its general arrangements, by the classification of its contents (mentioned hereafter), and by the beauty of its exhibits.

Twenty years ago, any one who should have dared to think of an exhibition almost immediately following upon another, would have been taxed with extraordinary temerity. A long time was then required for reflection before such a work was undertaken. The conquerors desired to enjoy their honours quietly for a time, and the vanquished prepared, at their leisure, new models of attack and of defence.

Now, men march with a much more rapid step. One combat finished, another is immediately commenced. The struggle is general and permanent. The victor of yesterday wants the laurels of to-morrow. The vanquished, sustained by a sense of his own valour, comes into the new arena with fresh powers, and a confidence more marked than ever. What, then, is our present position, after all this? In the long series of pacific combats, where rivalry is active without being hateful, where victory is glorious without being bloody, where even defeat is a title of esteem—in these competitions, born of peace and liberty, struggles of intelligence in the production of benefits and enjoyments for all mankind, we have never hands enough, and, resting upon the number of tools which form our arsenal, we repeat, in chorus, "to work! to work!"—while Paris, put to her wits' end to thoroughly satisfy all her visitors, says, by the thousands upon thousands of her inhabitants; "Come in, you are all welcome!" Rendezvous of all nations—connecting-link between England and America—she has to-day, more than ever, the right to say to every one: "Enter, study and amusement both invite you! Come and admire the *chefs d'œuvre* that the genius of man has caused to spring from the rapidity of his thought, as Jupiter of old created Minerva simply by striking his forehead."

But I am wandering—I am allowing myself to be led away by the charm of the scene which surrounds us. The fault is in the splendours which have been accumulated—in the happy grouping and arrangements. To say that the scene is fairy-like is to tell nothing. Nevertheless, I must restrain myself, and more especially so as the space at my command is now become very limited. So I shall simply append, in conclusion, a few descriptive and other miscellaneous notes—not omitting a list of the various "groups" and "classes" carefully registered in accordance with the official arrangements—which may prove useful or interesting to the Exhibition Visitor.

And now, with many wishes for your entertainment, and for a safe and easy journey back to the old land that we all love—the land where our affection, hope, and pride are centered—I cordially thank you for your company thus far, and wish you a hearty farewell.   C. M.

The great work for which France has strained every nerve in order to secure success, is now finished, and we may admire the definitive aspect of the Palace which crowns the summit of the Trocadéro. The domes have long since been covered in, and the central pavilion no longer has that depressing effect on the wings which was at first anticipated. Indeed, the general view of the Palace is imposing in the extreme. The interior fully corresponds in magnificence to the exterior. The grand festival hall is also finished, and the decorative work is very remarkable, the chief material employed being mosaic. Electric light will be used for the illumination of this great hall, capable of holding 8,000 persons. The whole of the foreign buildings in the park are completely terminated, and present a very handsome *coup d'œil*. The Aquarium—the subterranean palace of the fishes!—which will become the property of the City after the close of the Exhibition, has received its finny inhabitants, and the judicious obscurity which prevails there prepares us at once to admire the innumerable denizens of the wondrous ocean fields. On the Champ de Mars—the opposite side of the river—everything is ready also. The interior of the Palace, here, is devoted to the exhibits proper, for the facile examination of which a catalogue should be purchased in the building. This construction, in which elegance and chasteness of style are happily combined, is a masterpiece of ironwork, the *façades* of which are wrought into the most beautiful designs, characteristic of the respective styles of architecture of the different countries of the world. Its form is oblong, with a high dome flanking each of the four corners, and a central cupola rising from the principal entrance fronting the Pont d'Iéna and Trocadéro. This magnificent building is well worthy of the purpose to which it is devoted, and appears with honour among the many marvels which surround it on all sides.

The Grand Cascade of the Trocadéro is now completed, and must be acknowledged as a masterpiece of tasteful art. It has been constructed at a cost of 650,000 francs. Henceforward, the fountains and cascades of Versailles, St. Cloud, and Fontainebleau have a rival which likewise will play on Sundays and fête days. The Parisian cascade starts from under the centre of the Palace or Rotunda which commands the Trocodéro heights. From thence it descends, step by step, into the vast basin at the foot of the slope.

Ten grand concerts, with orchestra and choruses, will be given in the great hall of the Trocadéro during the Exhibition.

These concerts will be devoted to the execution of the works of French composers, and each of them will bear the name of some composer who has died since 1850. The composers chosen are: Adolphe Adam, Auber, Boïeldieu, Berlioz, Bizet, Chérubini, Félicien David, Halévy, Hérold, and Léon Kreutzer. A festival will be given on Sunday, July 21. A national competition will take place July 22. And an international one on the following day, July 23. In the month of September the festivals and competitions of the instrumental section will take place (harmonies and fanfares). The Musical Committee, which meets every week at the Conservatoire, has not yet fixed the dates for the orpheonic and other competitions.

The Paris Universal Exhibition of 1878 opened on the 1st of May, and will close on the last day of October. THE CHARGE FOR ADMITTANCE IS ONE FRANC. The Offices of the British Royal Commission are situated 40, Avenue de Suffren (Secretary, Mr. P. Cunliffe Owen, C.B.) The number of exhibitors exceeds 50,000, of whom 25,000 and upwards are for France alone.

At the present moment it is interesting to go back to the origin of an institution which has since been adopted by the whole civilized world. The first Industrial Exhibition took place in a shed in the court of the Louvre in the year 1798. The catalogue comprised four-and-twenty pages. Twenty silver medals and one single gold medal were offered to the manufacturers who should deal the heaviest blow to British trade. Native industry was, however, alone represented in the French Exhibition of 1798. A proposal was, indeed, made in 1849 that foreign products should be represented in the Paris Exhibition of that year; but the Minister of Commerce of the day was persuaded that such a project could only emanate from the enemies of French industry, and the suggestion fell to the ground. From the time that, in 1851, England acted on this broader principle, industrial exhibitions have increased in splendour and attractiveness. At London, in 1851, there were 13,917 exhibitors, 6,039,195 visitors, and the Exhibition was open 141 days. At Paris, in 1855, 23,954 exhibitors, 5,162,330 visitors, 200 days. At London, in 1862, 28,653 exhibitors, 6,211,103 visitors, 171 days. At Paris, in 1867, 50,226 exhibitors, 10,200,000 visitors, 210 days. At Vienna, in 1873, 42,584 exhibitors, 7,254,687 visitors, 186 days. At Philadelphia. in 1876, 9,857,625 visitors, 169 days.

The execution of the design for the diplomas of the Exhibition of 1878 has been entrusted to the celebrated painter

Paul Baudry, the decorator of the Grand Opera House. This design, which is now finished, represents France seated on a throne, leaning on Peace, and giving her hand to Labour, personified by a young man whose forehead is being touched by the finger of Genius.

LIST OF GROUPS, WITH THE CLASSES ABRIDGED.

Group I.—Works of Art.

Class 1. Oil Paintings.
 „ 2. Various Paintings and Drawings.
 „ 3. Sculpture and Die Sinking.
 „ 4. Architectural Drawings and Models.
 „ 5. Engravings and Lithographs.

Group II.—Education and Instruction—Apparatus and Processes of the Liberal Arts.

Class 6. Education of Children. Primary Instruction. Instruction of Adults.
 „ 7. Organization and Appliances for Secondary Instruction.
 „ 8. Organization, Methods, and Appliances for Superior Instruction.
 „ 9. Printing and Books.
 „ 10. Stationery, Bookbinding; Painting and Drawing Materials.
 „ 11. General Application of the Arts of Drawing and Modelling.
 „ 12. Photographic Proofs and Apparatus.
 „ 13. Musical Instruments.
 „ 14. Medicine, Hygiene, and Public Relief.
 „ 15. Mathematical and Philosophical Instruments.
 „ 16. Maps, and Geographical and Cosmographical Apparatus.

Group III.—Furniture and Accessories.

Class 17. Cheap and Fancy Furniture.
,, 18. Upholsterers' and Decorators' Work.
,, 19. Crystal, Glass, and Stained Glass.
,, 20. Pottery.
,, 21. Carpets, Tapestry, and other Stuffs for Furniture.
,, 22. Paper Hangings.
,, 23. Cutlery.
,, 24. Goldsmiths' and Silversmiths' Work.
,, 25. Bronzes, various Art Castings, and Repoussé Work.
,, 26. Clocks and Watches.
,, 27. Apparatus and Processes for Heating and Lighting.
,, 28. Perfumery.
,, 29. Leather Work, Fancy Articles, and Basket Work.

Group IV.—Textile Fabrics, Clothing and Accessories.

Class 30. Cotton Thread and Fabrics.
,, 31. Thread and Fabrics of Flax, Hemp, etc.
,, 32. Worsted Yarn and Fabrics.
,, 33. Woollen Yarn and Fabrics.
,, 34. Silk and Silk Fabrics.
,, 35. Shawls.
,, 36. Lace, Net, Embroidery, and Trimmings.
,, 37. Hosiery and Underclothing, and Accessories of Clothing.
,, 38. Clothing of both sexes.
,, 39. Jewellery and Precious Stones.
,, 40. Portable Weapons, and Hunting and Shooting Equipments.
,, 41. Travelling Apparatus, and Camp Equipage.
,, 42. Toys.

Group V.—Mining Industries, Raw and Manufactured Products.

Class 43. Mining and Metallurgy.
,, 44. Products of the Cultivation of Forests and of the Trades appertaining thereto.

Class 45. Products of Hunting, Shooting, Fishing, and Spontaneous Products, Machines and Instruments connected therewith.
„ 46. Agricultural Products not used for Food.
„ 47. Chemical and Pharmaceutical Products.
„ 48. Chemical Processes for Bleaching, Dyeing, Printing, and Dressing.
„ 49. Leather and Skins.

GROUP VI.—APPARATUS AND PROCESSES USED IN THE MECHANICAL MANUFACTURES.

Class 50. Apparatus and Processes of the Art of Mining and Metallurgy.
„ 51. Agricultural Implements, and Processes used in the Cultivation of Fields and Forests.
„ 52. Apparatus and Processes used in Agricultural Works, and in Works for the Preparation of Food.
„ 53. Apparatus used in Chemistry, Pharmacy, and Tanning.
„ 54. Machines and Apparatus in general.
„ 55. Machine Tools.
„ 56. Apparatus and Processes used in Spinning and Rope making.
„ 57. Apparatus and Processes used in Weaving.
„ 58. Apparatus and Processes for Sewing and for making up Clothing.
„ 59. Apparatus and Processes used in the Manufacture of Furniture and Objects for Dwellings.
„ 60. Apparatus and Processes used in Paper making, Dyeing, and Printing.
„ 61. Machines, Instruments, and Processes used in various works.
„ 62. Carriages and Wheelwrights' Work.
„ 63. Harness and Saddlery.
„ 64. Railway Apparatus.
„ 65. Telegraphic Apparatus and Processes.
„ 66. Apparatus and Processes of Civil Engineering, Public Works, and Architecture.
„ 67. Apparatus for Navigation and Life Saving.
„ 68. Materials and Apparatus for Military purposes.

Group VII.—Alimentary Products.

Class 69. Cereals, Farinaceous Products, and Products derived from them.
,, 70. Bread and Pastry.
,, 71. Fatty Substances used as Food. Milk and Eggs.
,, 72. Meat and Fish.
,, 73. Vegetables and Fruit.
,, 74. Condiments and Stimulants, Sugar and Confectionery.
,, 75. Fermented Drinks.

Group VIII.—Agriculture and Pisciculture.

Class 76. Specimens of Farm Buildings and Agricultural Works.
,, 77. Horses, Donkeys, Mules, etc.
,, 78. Oxen, Buffaloes, etc.
,, 79. Sheep, Goats.
,, 80. Pigs, Rabbits, etc.
,, 81. Poultry.
,, 82. Dogs.
,, 83. Useful Insects and Noxious Insects.
,, 84. Fish, Crustacea, and Mollusca.

Group IX.—Horticulture.

Class 85. Conservatories and Horticultural Apparatus.
,, 86. Flowers and Ornamental Plants.
,, 87. Vegetables.
,, 88. Fruit and Fruit Trees.
,, 89. Seeds and Saplings of Forest Trees.
,, 90. Plants for Conservatories.

THERMOMETER.

While Fahrenheit's scale is generally used in England, that of Réaumur is in vogue on the Continent. The following Table will show the difference of the two Thermometers, and also the comparison of these with the Centigrade :—

Réaumur.	Centigrade.	Fahrenheit.	Réaumur.	Centigrade.	Fahrenheit.
80	100	212 Boiling.	24	30	86
76	95	203	20	25	77
72	90	194	19	24	75 Summer.
68	85	185	16	20	68
64	80	176	12	15	59
60	75	167	10	13	55 Temperate.
56	70	158	8	10	50
52	65	149	4	5	41
48	60	140	3	4	39
44	55	131	2	3	37
40	50	122	1	2	35
36	45	113	0.8	1	33
36	45	112 Fever.	0.0	0	32 Freezing.
32	40	104	·4	·5	23
29	37	98 Blood.	·8	·10	14
28	35	95	·12.	·15	5

CALENDAR FOR 1878.

JANUARY.	FEBRUARY.	MARCH.	APRIL.
S M T W T F S	S M T W T F S	S M T W T F S	S M T W T F S
... 1 2 3 4 5	... ... 1 2	... ... 1 2	... 1 2 3 4 5 6
6 7 8 9 10 11 12	3 4 5 6 7 8 9	3 4 5 6 7 8 9	7 8 9 10 11 12 13
13 14 15 16 17 18 19	10 11 12 13 14 15 16	10 11 12 13 14 15 16	14 15 16 17 18 19 20
20 21 22 23 24 25 26	17 18 19 20 21 22 23	17 18 19 20 21 22 23	21 22 23 24 25 26 27
27 28 29 30 31 ...	24 25 26 27 28	24 25 26 27 28 29 30 / 31	28 29 30 ... ...

MAY.	JUNE.	JULY.	AUGUST.
S M T W T F S	S M T W T F S	S M T W T F S	S M T W T F S
... ... 1 2 3 4	 1	... 1 2 3 4 5 6	... ... 1 2 3
5 6 7 8 9 10 11	2 3 4 5 6 7 8	7 8 9 10 11 12 13	4 5 6 7 8 9 10
12 13 14 15 16 17 18	9 10 11 12 13 14 15	14 15 16 17 18 19 20	11 12 13 14 15 16 17
19 20 21 22 23 24 25	16 17 18 19 20 21 22	21 22 23 24 25 26 27	18 19 20 21 22 23 24
26 27 28 29 30 31 ...	23 24 25 26 27 28 29 / 30	28 29 30 31	25 26 27 28 29 30 31

SEPTEMBER.	OCTOBER.	NOVEMBER.	DECEMBER.
S M T W T F S	S M T W T F S	S M T W T F S	S M T W T F S
1 2 3 4 5 6 7	... ... 1 2 3 4 5	... ... 1 2	1 2 3 4 5 6 7
8 9 10 11 12 13 14	6 7 8 9 10 11 12	3 4 5 6 7 8 9	8 9 10 11 12 13 14
15 16 17 18 19 20 21	13 14 15 16 17 18 19	10 11 12 13 14 15 16	15 16 17 18 19 20 21
22 23 24 25 26 27 28	20 21 22 23 24 25 26	17 18 19 20 21 22 23	22 23 24 25 26 27 28
29 30	27 28 29 30 31	24 25 26 27 28 29 30	29 30 31 ... ...

Cook's Exhibition Boarding House,

24 AND 26, RUE DE LA FAISANDERIE.

(Avenue d'Eylau.)

These premises are situated in one of the most beautiful and well-known districts of Paris, within eleven minutes of the Exhibition, and three minutes of the entrance to the Bois de Boulogne.

MODES OF CONVEYANCE.

OMNIBUS ROUTE from the **Bourse** (centre of Paris) to **Passy**, *via* the Boulevarts, Madeleine, Palace of the Elysée, Arc de Triomphe, and Avenue d'Eylau. These omnibuses run about every five minutes in each direction, from 7.30 a.m. to 11.30 p.m. The price is 30 c. for the inside places and 15 c. for the outside. Care should be taken to tell the conductor on paying to stop his vehicle at the corner of Rue de Longchamps (to the right of Avenue d'Eylau). From here it is only five hundred paces to Rue de la Faisanderie, *via* Rue Spontini to the right of Rue de Longchamps, and Rue Benouville to the left, which leads direct to Cook's Boarding House. The drive between the omnibus station of the Madeleine and the Rue de Longchamps is very pleasant, and lasts half an hour.

RAILWAY ROUTE from the **Gare St. Lazare** (Place du Hâvre, opposite Cook's Tourist Office) to the **Avenue du Bois de Boulogne**, crossing on the way the stations of Batignolles, Courcelles, and Porte Maillot. Trains every half hour, from 6.30 a.m. till 9.30 p.m. Fares on weekdays: 1st class 40 c., 2nd class 30 c. On Sundays and fête days: 1st class 65 c., 2nd class 45 c. Time of journey: fourteen minutes. The Rue de la Faisanderie is the first turning to the right from the station of the Metropolitan Railway (*Chemin de fer de Ceinture*).

COOK'S "FOUR-IN-HAND" EXCURSIONS
IN PARIS AND ITS ENVIRONS.
PERSONALLY CONDUCTED BY MR. CHARLES MOONEN.

FIRST EXCURSION. (Mondays, Tuesdays, Thursdays, and Fridays.)

New French Opera, Grand Boulevarts, Madeleine, Place de la Concorde and Obelisk of Luxor, Champs Elysées, Palace of Industry, Palace of the Elysée, Arc de Triomphe de l'Etoile, Exhibition Buildings, Ecole Militaire, Invalides and Tomb of Napoleon, Ministry of Foreign Affairs, Palace Bourbon, Pont de la Concorde, Palace of the Legion of Honour, Palace of the Council of State (ruins), Tuileries, Palais Royal.

LUNCHEON.

Bibliothèque Nationale, Bourse, Rue de Lafayette, Square Montholon, St. Vincent de Paul, Northern Railway Terminus, Park of the Buttes Chaumont, Cemetery of Père La Chaise, Prison de la Roquette and Place of Execution, Place de la Bastille and Column of July, Place du Château d'Eau, Porte St. Martin, Porte St. Denis, La Trinité.

SECOND EXCURSION. (Daily, Mondays excepted.)

St. Augustin, Park Monceau, Arc de Triomphe, Bois de Boulogne, the Lakes, Grand Cascade, and Racecourse, View of the Citadel of Mont Valérien, Town and Park of St. Cloud, Montretout-Buzenval, Forest of Ville d'Avray, Avenue de Picardie, Versailles, the Grand Trianon and State Carriages.

LUNCHEON.

Palace, Museum, and **Park of Versailles**, Avenue de Paris, Viroflay, Chaville, Sèvres and its Porcelain Manufactory (exterior), Billancourt, Fortifications of Paris, Viaduct of Auteuil, Palace of the Trocadéro, Seine Embankment, Cours La Reine.

THIRD EXCURSION. (Wednesdays and Saturdays.)

Column Vendôme, Garden of the Tuileries, Institute of France, Mint, Pont Neuf and Statue of Henry IV., Palace of

Justice, Ste. Chapelle, Tribunal of Commerce, Conciergerie, Cour de Cassation, St. Germain l'Auxerrois, Palace and Museum of the Louvre, Palais Royal.

LUNCHEON.

Place du Carrousel and Triumphal Arch, Ecole des Beaux Arts, St. Germain des Prés, St. Sulpice, Palace of the Luxembourg, St. Jacques du Haut Pas, Val de Grâce, Carpet Manufactory of the Gobelins, Observatory, Statue of Marshal Ney, Fountain and Gardens of the Luxembourg, Panthéon, Bibliothèque Ste. Geneviève, St. Etienne du Mont, Fontaine Cuvier, Jardin des Plantes, Orleans Railway Terminus, Halle aux Vins, Morgue, Cathedral of Notre Dame, Hôtel Dieu, Place du Châtelet, the new Avenue de l'Opéra.

FOURTH EXCURSION. (Mondays only.)

Grand Boulevarts, St. Ambroise, Place du Trône, Cours de Vincennes, Fortifications of Paris, Donjon, Fort, and Forest of Vincennes, Redoubt of La Faisanderie, Joinville Le Pont, Battlefields of Champigny, the Ruins, Monument, and Prussian Cemeteries, Panorama of Paris, Joinville.

LUNCHEON.

Valley of the Marne, Redoubt of La Gravelle, Polygone of Vincennes, St. Mandé, Prison Mazas, Lyons Railway Terminus, Place de la Bastille, St. Paul, St. Gervais, Hôtel de Ville (rebuilding), Tower of St. Jacques La Boucherie, Rue de Rivoli.

Fares.—For One Excursion, 8s.; for the first Three Excursions, 21s. (including everything except lunch). The new "four-in-hand" carriages start *precisely* at 10 a.m. from Cook's Tourist Office, 15, Place du Hâvre, and from Cook's Boarding House, 24, Rue de la Faisanderie, and return about 5.30 p.m. These splendid carriages have been constructed with the utmost care as regards workmanship and comfort.

Tickets for all the above Excursions can be obtained of THOS. COOK & SON, Ludgate Circus, London, or at any of their Branch Offices; and may also be procured the previous day (before 6 p.m.) at the Paris Office, 15, Place du Hâvre, and at the Exhibition Boarding House, 24, Rue de la Faisanderie.

INDEX.

	PAGE
Abattoirs	28
Arc de Triomphe du Carroussel	28
„ „ de l'Etoile	28
Ambassadors	12
Amusements, Public	16
Artesian Well	66
Asnières	75
Bank of France	29
Bankers	10
Bastille	60
Battlefields	74
Bibliothèque Nationale	29
„ Ste. Geneviève	30
Boarding House, Cook's	93
Bois de Boulogne	30
Boulevarts	30
Bourget (Le)	75
Bourse	31
Buttes Chaumont	31
Buzenval	75
Cabs	10
Cafes	11
Calendar for 1878	92
Carriages, Four in Hand	94
„ State	81
Catacombs	32
Cathedral of Notre Dame	50
Cemetery of Père La Chaise	58
Champ de Mars	33
Champs Elysées	33
Champigny	75
Chapelle Expiatoire	34
Chapels, Protestant	12

	PAGE
Châtelet	61
Church of the Madeleine	48
„ St. Ambroise	66
„ St. Augustin	66
„ St. Etienne du Mont	66
„ St. Eustache	67
„ St. Germain l'Auxerrois	67
„ „ des Prés	68
„ St. Gervais	68
„ St. Jacques du Haut Pas	68
„ St. Laurent	68
„ St. Paul	68
„ St. Roch	69
„ St. Sulpice	69
„ St. Vincent de Paul	69
„ Ste. Clotilde	70
„ Ste. Geneviève	55
„ of the Sorbonne	71
„ of the Trinité	72
„ of the Val de Grâce	73
Churches, Protestant	12
Cluny, Museum of	50
Colonne de Juillet	34
„ Vendôme	34
Commune of 1871, Incidents of the	29, 30, 32, 33, 34, 35, 36, 38, 41, 44, 46, 48, 49, 50, 52, 54, 55, 60, 61, 62, 64, 65, 70, 71, 73, 75, 77, 83
Compiègne	76
Conciergerie	35
Concorde	62
Conseil d'Etat	52

INDEX.

	PAGE
Conservatoire des Arts et Métiers.	35
Consulates	12
Cook's Excursions around and about Paris	94
„ Exhibition Boarding House	93
Cour de Cassation	35
Divine Services, Protestant	12
Drives, Four-in-Hand.	94
Ecole des Beaux Arts	36
„ Militaire	36
Embassies	12
Enghien	77
Environs of Paris	75
Exchange	31
Excursions, Four-in-Hand	94
Exhibition, Great Universal, 1878 5, 14, 18, 33, 84	
Faisanderie, Rue de la	93
Fiacres	10
Fontainebleau	77
Fortifications of Paris.	38
Fountain Cuvier.	37
„ des Innocents	37
„ du Luxembourg	37
„ Molière	38
„ St. Michel	37
„ St. Sulpice	38
Four-in-Hand Excursions	94
Gardens 31, 37, 44, 45, 54, 55, 57, 71, 72, 81	
Gobelins	38
Halle au Blé	39
„ aux Vins	39
Halles Centrales	39
History of Paris	7
Hotel, Cook's Exhibition	93
„ Dieu	40
„ des Monnaies	40
„ des Postes	40
„ de Ville	41
Institute of France	41
Invalides	42
Jardin d'Acclimatation	44
„ du Luxembourg	44
„ des Plantes	45
„ des Tuileries	45
Joinville	77
Légion d'Honneur	54
Lodgings—see "Boarding House"	
Louvre	46
Luxembourg	47

	PAGE
Madeleine	48
Markets	39
Measures	14
Metropolitan Railway	13
Mileage Table	15
Ministry of Foreign Affairs	49
Mint	40
Monetary System	14
Mont Valérien	77
Morgue	49
Museum of Cluny	50
„ of the Louvre	47
„ of the Luxembourg	48
Napoleon's Tomb	43
Newspapers	15
Notre Dame	50
Obelisk of Luxor	62
Observatory	51
Omnibuses	16
Opera	51
Palace Bourbon.	52
„ du Conseil d'Etat	52
„ de l'Elysée	53
„ de l'Industrie	53
„ de Justice	53
„ de la Légion d'Honneur	54
„ du Louvre	46
„ du Luxembourg	47
„ Royal	54
„ des Thermes	55
„ du Trocadéro	6, 86
„ des Tuileries	72
Panorama	33
Panthéon	55
Paris, Alphabetical Description of	28
Park Monceau	57
Père La Chaise	58
Place de la Bastille	60
„ du Carrousel	61
„ du Château d'Eau	61
„ du Châtelet	61
„ de la Concorde	62
„ of Public Execution	65
„ du Trône	63
„ des Victoires	63
Places of Amusement	16
Pont Neuf	63
Population of Paris	28
Porte St. Denis	64
„ St. Martin	64
Post Office	40

INDEX.

	PAGE
Prison Mazas	65
„ de la Roquette	65
Programme of Cook's Excursions	94
Railways	13, 17
Restaurants	17
Rotunda of the Trocadéro	86
Rue de la Faisanderie	93
St. Ambroise	66
St. Augustin	66
St. Cloud	78
St. Denis	79
St. Etienne du Mont	66
St. Eustache	67
St. Germain	79
„ l'Auxerrois	67
„ des Prés	68
St. Gervais	68
St. Jacques du Haut Pas	68
St. Laurent	68
St. Paul	68
St. Roch	69
St. Sulpice	69
St. Vincent de Paul	69
Ste. Chapelle	70
Ste. Clotilde	70
Ste. Geneviève	55
Sèvres	80
Sieges of Paris—*See Commune, War*	

	PAGE
Sorbonne	70
State Carriages	81
Statue of Henry IV.	64
„ Louis XIV.	63
„ Marshal Ney	71
Steamboats	18
Theatres	18
Thermometer	92
Tomb of Napoleon	43
Tower of St. Jacques	71
Tramways	16
Trianons	81
Tribunal of Commerce	72
Trinité (La)	72
Trips, Four-in-Hand	94
Trocadéro	6, 86
Tuileries	72
University of Paris	70
Val de Grâce	73
Versailles	80
Vincennes	82
Vocabulary of Useful Words	20
War of 1870—71, Incidents of the 30, 33, 38, 44, 46, 49, 57, 62, 67, 73, 75, 76, 77, 78, 79, 80, 81, 82	
Weights	14
Zoological Gardens	44, 45

Appendix.

MESSRS. THOS. COOK & SON'S APPOINTMENT AS PASSENGER AGENTS.

LONDON, 1st *November*, 1877.

GENTLEMEN,

I am directed by His Royal Highness the Prince of Wales, President of the Royal Commission for the Paris Universal Exhibition of 1878, to inform you that, in consideration of the services which you rendered to the British Executive throughout the Vienna Exhibition of 1873, you have been appointed Exhibitors' Passenger-Agents for the British Section of the Paris Exhibition.

The principal object which His Royal Highness has in view is the reduction of the Passenger Rates in favour specially of the Exhibitors, their Assistants and Workmen, who may be visiting Paris throughout the course of the next year.

The arrangements which you so successfully made for the Vienna Exhibition render it a matter of very great importance, and one in which His Royal Highness is personally interested, to provide the greatest possible facilities and the largest reductions for the benefit of the large number of Exhibitors, who at the invitation of His Royal Highness are taking part in the Exhibition.

I am,

Gentlemen,

Your obedient servant,

(*Signed*) P. CUNLIFFE OWEN.

Messrs. THOS. COOK & SON,
Ludgate Circus, London.

TRAVELLING, HOTEL AND BOARDING HOUSE ARRANGEMENTS.

Messrs. THOS. COOK & SON

Originators of the British and European Excursion and Tourist system, respectfully invite the attention of all classes of the community to the following outline of their extensive arrangements for visiting Paris during the Exhibition season of 1878.

On the occasion of the Paris Exhibition of 1867, the travelling arrangements of Messrs. T. C. & SON were exclusively *via* the Newhaven and Dieppe route, under which arrangements they had the pleasure of booking to Paris over 20,000 passengers, many being brought by special trains from all parts of Great Britain. Since 1867, Messrs. T. C. & SON have deemed it advisable, in the interests of all concerned, to enter into arrangements with the London Chatham and Dover Company for the conveyance of their passengers who wish to take the

SHORT SEA MAIL ROUTE, via DOVER AND CALAIS,

to be able to do so. And as Excursion Agents for the Midland Railway Company, in which capacity Messrs. T. C. & SON advertise the *whole of the Excursions by Midland route to London* from Edinboro', Glasgow, Dublin, Belfast, Liverpool, Manchester, Leeds, Bradford, Sheffield, Birmingham, Nottingham, Derby, Leicester, and all other chief stations in connection with the Midland system, Messrs. T. C. & SON issue on behalf of the Midland Railway Company tickets from

ALL PARTS OF GREAT BRITAIN AVAILABLE FROM LONDON BY ALL ROUTES TO PARIS.

This programme is issued for the purpose of giving a brief outline of the extensive and various facilities and arrangements provided by Messrs. T. C. & SON, combining the cheapest and most expensive routes with the Hotel and Boarding House arrangements in Paris, or, leaving the travellers with Messrs. T. C. & SON'S Tickets at perfect liberty to select their own accommodation in Paris. As the question of expense of living in Paris during the Exhibition season will be of more serious importance than the cost of the journey to and from Paris, priority is herewith given to the cost of living in Paris, varying from 6s. to 24s. per day.

For the protection of passengers to previous Exhibitions in London during 1862, and in Paris during 1867, Mr. THOS. COOK felt compelled to take upon himself the responsibility of providing establishments under his

APPENDIX. 101

own control at reasonable charges. And as Messrs. T. C. & SON find that the Hotel proprietors of Paris are compelled, through extra cost of all articles consumed, and through extra taxation, to advance their charges about 50 per cent. during the coming Exhibition, Messrs. T. C. & SON feel they have no alternative but to incur heavy pecuniary responsibilities by establishing their own

COOK'S EXHIBITION BOARDING HOUSE

(For the exclusive use of travellers to Paris with Cook's Tickets), capable of accommodating about 90 persons, and, adjoining the same, sleeping accommodation for 200 other visitors. The premises are situated in one of the most beautiful and best known districts of Paris, close to the Bois de Boulogne Railway Station, within ten minutes from the Place du Havre, within a fifteen minutes' walk by a new direct boulevard to the Exhibition, and within five minutes' walk of the entrance to the Bois de Boulogne—a locality in which 12,000 visitors to the Exhibition of 1867 were accommodated by Mr. THOS. COOK.

In reference to the accommodation of this Establishment, the principles successfully adopted in London in 1862, and in Paris in 1867, will be repeated. In the BOARDING HOUSE proper, bedroom for one or more persons, on first, second, or third floors, with lights; breakfast of hot or cold meats, eggs, tea, or coffee, at 6s. to 8s. per day, according to character of rooms. Tea, with or without meat, will be supplied in the evening, at extra charges of 1s. for plain tea, and 2s. for tea and hot or cold meats. In this department 6d. per day will be charged for attendance, boot cleaning and house porterage (not including messages and services *outside the house*, for which a reasonable charge will be made). Sitting rooms extra.

In the SECOND DEPARTMENT, including the top floor of the Boarding House and the new rooms erected for the occasion, provision will be made for both sexes apart, and for married couples. The rooms will contain two, three, or four single beds. In a large room, built for the occasion, will be supplied—breakfast, consisting of cold roast or boiled beef, etc., best English ham and eggs, with tea or coffee, at a charge of 4s. or 5s. per day (according to room accommodation), and 3d. per day extra for attendance, boot cleaning, and house porterage. In the evening, at fixed hours, hot meat will be served with tea or coffee, and at any time, tea, with or without cold meat, can be had. Prices, plain tea or coffee, with bread and butter, one franc (10d.); plate of meat, one franc. Other light refreshments as per tariff. Our dinners will thus be "Tea Dinners," or, as designated in Scotland, "Tea and Eating."

These arrangements will be under the personal superintendence of Mr. THOMAS COOK, and the houses will be opened to commence business at Easter.

HOTELS IN PARIS.

It is not necessary in this programme to give a full list of all the hotels Messrs. THOS. COOK & SON have their special contracts with for the Exhibition season; but to enable intending passengers to form an estimate of the probable cost of their visit to Paris, it may be stated that the hotel charges vary from 10s. to 24s. per day (according to the class of hotel) for bed, lights and service, meat breakfast, and dinner at *table d'hote*. The

APPENDIX.

charges at the Grand Hotel include plain breakfast, and *déjeuner a la fourchette*, so providing an extra meal.

For the Exhibition Season of 1878 (as in 1867) it will be absolutely necessary for intending visitors to register their names, and thus secure their rooms as far in advance as possible; and as a system of registration involves considerable extra labour and correspondence, Messrs. T. C. & SON will be compelled, as in 1867, to charge a registration fee of 1s. per passenger, in addition to the charge for hotel or boarding-house. Cards will be issued for any number of days' accommodation the passenger may require.

It must be distinctly understood that Messrs. T. C. & SON will issue at all their offices, tickets for the journey to Paris and back, quite independently of Hotel or Boarding House arrangements; but in no case will they register visitors for Hotels or Boarding House, unless they purchase the travelling tickets of Messrs. T. C. & SON, or their appointed agents and representatives.

THE RAILWAY ARRANGEMENTS

Of Messrs T. C. & SON will be of such a nature as to meet the requirements of all classes of society, "from Prince to Peasant," and will enable

ONE OR MORE PASSENGERS TO TRAVEL BY ANY ROUTE ANY DAY,

Breaking their journey at chief points of interest, according to the route selected.

PRIVATE FAMILY OR FRIENDLY PARTIES

Of 20 or upwards, will be provided with a Special Conductor between London and Paris, without extra cost, by giving at least 7 days' clear notice to the Chief Office, Ludgate Circus, London.

PERSONALLY CONDUCTED PARTIES,

At inclusive Fares, providing for accommodation in Hotels or Cook's Exhibition Boarding House, carriage drives to all points of interest in and around Paris, fees for sight-seeing, admission to the Exhibition, and services of Conductor, will be arranged to leave London every week by each route.

CHEAP SPECIAL EXCURSIONS,

Commencing at Whitsuntide, will be run every fortnight. These Excursions will be worked by special services of trains and steamers, and will be accompanied throughout by Messrs. T. C. & SON'S Interpreters and Conductors.

ARTIZANS, CLUBS, SOCIETIES, &c., &c.,

Will be conveyed and provided for under special arrangements, in accordance with the numbers and requirements of the different Societies.

APPENDIX.

CARRIAGE EXCURSIONS IN AND AROUND PARIS

Will be made a special department under the management of one of Messrs. T. C. & SON's chief representatives, assisted by a staff of Guides, thoroughly conversant with Paris, and its history. Two distinct classes of Carriage Excursions will be organized, one in superior carriages at the same rates as in previous years, and another exclusively for passengers booked from England under the cheap personally conducted party arrangements.

These arrangements will be advertised at inclusive fares, and Messrs. T. C. & SON positively prohibit their assistants or guides from receiving fees or further payment from the passengers.

INTERPRETERS, OMNIBUSES TO AND FROM HOTELS, &c.

Messrs. T. C. & SON purpose increasing their staff of Interpreters, so that one will be in attendance to meet every "Boat-Train" on its arrival in Paris, and every passenger with "Cook's Tickets" will be entitled to their assistance and information. Omnibuses, specially retained for Cook's passengers, will also be regularly worked between the Railway Stations and Hotels and Boarding Houses.

PRIVATE HOUSES OR APARTMENTS IN PARIS.

In order to meet the wishes of those who may desire to engage furnished houses, or suites of apartments for families during the Exhibition Season, Messrs. THOMAS COOK & SON have made Special Arrangements by which they are enabled to secure such accommodation. Letters of enquiry should state the number of rooms required; whether with or without board; the quarter of Paris preferred; and the maximum amount of rent that would be paid. The latter information is required as a guide to the style of houses or apartments required. The houses and apartments will be let for three months and upwards.

For further particulars apply to

THOS. COOK & SON.

CHIEF OFFICE—LUDGATE CIRCUS, LONDON.
PARIS OFFICE—15, PLACE DU HAVRE.

EXHIBITION OFFICE—British Section, near Machinery Department.
TROCADERO OFFICE—Opposite the entrance to the Trocadero.
BOARDING HOUSE OFFICE—24, Rue de la Faisanderie.
At all of which full information will be given and Tickets issued.

For more detailed particulars of all the above arrangements, see Cook's Paris Exhibition Programme, which gives Fares, Routes, etc. To be obtained at any of the Offices and Agencies of THOS. COOK & SON.

Memoranda.

Memoranda.

Memoranda.

MIDLAND RAILWAY.

The Picturesque and Favourite Route between London and Manchester and Liverpool, and all Parts of Lancashire, via Matlock and the Peak of Derbyshire.

THE NEW TOURIST AND EXCURSION ROUTE between ENGLAND and SCOTLAND, via SETTLE and CARLISLE, is now Open, and a Service of Express and Fast Trains is run between LONDON and EDINBURGH and GLASGOW, with connections and through Booking Arrangements from principal Stations in the West of England, Midland Counties, Yorkshire and Lancashire, and principal towns and places of Tourist resort in Scotland.

The Trains to Glasgow run to the St. Enoch Station, via Dumfries, and through the Land of Burns; and those to Edinburgh run by the Waverley Route, via Melrose and the Land of Scott.

PULLMAN DRAWING-ROOM CARS by day and SLEEPING CARS by night are run between London and Manchester, Liverpool, Edinburgh, and Glasgow; and PULLMAN DRAWING-ROOM CARS are also run by certain trains between London and Sheffield and Leeds, Bristol and Birmingham, and Birmingham and Leeds.

PARIS EXHIBITION.

The Midland Company Book passengers through to PARIS from all principal Stations on their line of Railway, for Particulars of which, see their Official Time Tables. CHEAP EXCURSIONS will be arranged from the Midland system to Paris at frequent intervals during the continuance of the Exhibition.

TOURIST TICKETS,

Available for Two Calendar Months, are issued during the summer months from principal Stations on the Midland Railway to Edinburgh, Glasgow, and all parts of Scotland, The Lake District, Scarboro', and the North-East Coast, Matlock, Buxton, North and South Wales, and the South and West of England, Isle of Wight, &c. For Particulars, see Tourist Programmes.

DERBY, *April*, 1878.

JAMES ALLPORT,
General Manager.

ARUNDEL PRIVATE HOTEL,
13, 14, 19, 20, & 26, ARUNDEL STREET, STRAND, LONDON.

Passengers travelling from any part of the NORTH, SOUTH, or WEST of ENGLAND can arrive at the TEMPLE STATION (NEXT DOOR to this Hotel).

At this ESTABLISHMENT, now the largest of the kind in London, and situate on the NEW VICTORIA EMBANKMENT, the Charge including Breakfast, Luncheon, Dinner (5 courses), and Tea, a good Bedroom, and use of well-appointed Sitting-rooms,

SIX SHILLINGS AND SIXPENCE PER DAY.

This Hotel is largely patronised by Professional Men, Officers of both Services and their Families, for whom it is especially adapted, the Rooms being large and scrupulously clean. Private Sitting-rooms, from 3s. per day. Service, 1s. No other extras. An elegantly appointed Suite of Rooms appropriated for Wedding Breakfasts. Hot and Cold Baths. A Night Porter. Ici on parle Français. Man spricht Deutsch.

THE CALEDONIAN HOTEL,
ADELPHI TERRACE, STRAND, LONDON.

THIS OLD-ESTABLISHED FIRST-CLASS HOTEL, under new Management, overlooks the Thames Embankment, is close to the CHARING CROSS TERMINUS, and in proximity to the Houses of Parliament, Law Courts, Clubs, and Theatres. It has been recently redecorated, and amongst many improvements an elegant LADIES' COFFEE ROOM has been added, and the Bedroom accommodation considerably enlarged. In the Spacious Dining Room, facing the River, a TABLE D'HOTE of a Recherche Character (6 courses) is given daily at 6 p.m., at the moderate charge of Two Shillings and Sixpence.

PRIVATE SITTING ROOMS FROM 3s. PER DAY.
ATTENDANCE, 1s.; NO OTHER EXTRAS.
Permanent Residents can have Full Board and Apartments at 7s. 0d. per Day.

A Night Porter. On parle Français. Man spricht Deutsch. Si parla Italiano.

THE
HOLBORN RESTAURANT,
218, HIGH HOLBORN.

ONE OF THE SIGHTS AND ONE OF THE COMFORTS OF LONDON.

ATTRACTIONS OF THE CHIEF PARISIAN ESTABLISHMENTS, WITH THE QUIET AND ORDER ESSENTIAL TO ENGLISH CUSTOMS.

Dinners and Luncheons from Daily Bill of Fare.

A TABLE D'HOTE AT SEPARATE TABLES,
EVERY EVENING,

IN THE GRAND SALON, THE PRINCE'S SALON, AND THE DUKE'S SALON,

From 6 to 8.30, 3s. 6d.

INCLUDING

TWO SOUPS, TWO KINDS OF FISH, TWO ENTREES, JOINTS, SWEETS, CHEESE (IN VARIETY), SALAD &c., WITH ICES AND DESSERT.

This favourite Dinner is accompanied by a Selection of high-class Instrumental Music.

Single Seats or Tables may be engaged by Letter or Telegram addressed to the Manager.

THE
SOUTH PLACE HOTEL
(PRIVATE, FAMILY, & COMMERCIAL),
FINSBURY, LONDON, E.C.

Is unsurpassed for its central position and easy access from all parts of the kingdom; having also a high reputation of twenty years, for thorough comfort in every department, as a First-class Temperance Hotel.

SUITES OF ROOMS.	COFFEE ROOM.
Drawing Room, with Bedroom en suite - - - 8/0 to 12/0	Breakfasts - - - - 1/6 to 2/6
Service, 1/6 per day.	Dinners - - - - 2/0 to 3/0
Ground Floor Bedrooms - 2/6 to 5/0	Bedrooms - - - - 1/6 to 3/0
	Service, 1/0 per day.

This Hotel having been again considerably enlarged, contains lofty and excellent

COFFEE, COMMERCIAL, AND PRIVATE SITTING-ROOMS.

With about Fifty thoroughly Clean, Well-appointed, and Airy Bedrooms.
A NIGHT PORTER IN ATTENDANCE.

JOSEPH ARMFIELD, Proprietor.

N.B.—Three minutes' walk from BROAD STREET, LIVERPOOL STREET, and MOORGATE STATIONS.

J. STROHMENGER & SONS'
PIANOFORTES

Iron Frames, overstrung for all Climates, excellence of Tone and durability of the mechanism warranted.

Show Rooms,
206, GOSWELL ROAD, LONDON.

On the Three Years' System of Hire, from 15s. per Month till purchased.

7 octaves, trichord, check action.

Manufactory,
169, GOSWELL ROAD, LONDON.

And at the Paris Exhibition (English Section).

COOK'S
BRITISH MUSEUM BOARDING HOUSE,
59, GREAT RUSSELL STREET, BLOOMSBURY.
(OPPOSITE THE BRITISH MUSEUM.)

THIS ESTABLISHMENT is pleasantly situated within three minutes' walk of Oxford Street and High Holborn, the great Omnibus route to the City and the West End, with easy facilities for visiting every part of the Metropolis.

TURIN.
HOTEL TROMBETTA,
In the finest quarter of the town, at the corner of the Roma and Cavour Streets, in the neighbourhood of the Porta Nuova Station.

Proprietor, LEOPOLD BAGLIONI.

The Hotel has been entirely and newly fitted up with great luxury, and according to the latest improvements. It now, more than ever, offers the most desirable residence to English travellers visiting this fine climate. Suites of apartments for families, and elegant well-furnished rooms for single gentlemen. Conversation, reading, and smoking rooms. Excellent accommodation, combined with reasonable terms. Foreign newspapers. Baths. Omnibuses at the station. Arrangements made for a protracted stay. Cook's Coupons accepted here.

MILAN.
GRAND HOTEL DE MILAN,
Corso del Guardino.

J. SPATZ, Proprietor.

This first-class establishment is entirely restored by the new proprietors, and fitted up in the most comfortable style. It contains Two Hundred Rooms, large and small Apartments for families and single gentlemen, and is very well situated in the centre of the Railway Stations, Public Gardens, Cathedral, Theatre Scala, Picture Gallery, etc. Table d'Hote, Breakfast, Lunch, and Dinner at any hour, at fixed prices, or à la carte. Music Saloon, Reading-room, Smoking room. Hot and Cold Baths. Moderate Charges. Lift in communication with each storey.

BELLAGIO, ON THE LAKE OF COMO (ITALY).
GRAND HOTEL BELLAGIO.
L. BREITSCHMIDT, Manager.

One of the finest Hotels in Europe, situated on one of the most beautiful parts of the Lake, and surrounded by a splendid Garden and Park. Superior accommodation. Thirty Sitting-rooms. Saloons. Fine Dining-room, and every comfort combined with moderate charges. N.B.—The Hotel is patronised by the high class of English and American travellers.

TO TOURISTS.
MONTHLY TRACT SOCIETY,
5, New Bridge Street, Blackfriars, Opposite Ludgate Hill Railway Station.

A SALOON has been opened, where the publications of the Society may be seen every day from Ten till Five, except on Saturdays, when it closes at One o'clock. Every information, with Price and List of publications, may be obtained of the Secretary, Mr. JOHN STABB.

RECENT PUBLICATIONS.—TRACTS FOR ADULTS.
The Bible, is it of God or Man?—Spiritual Bondage.—The Christ of the Gospels.—Sir Titus Salt, Bart.—Sunrise on the Rigi.—Life and Liberty.—General Macartney's Victory.

FOR CHILDREN.
The Little Heiress.—Walter's Difficulty.—Millie's Dream.—What can I do?—Lost on the Shore.—The Old Abbey.
A Tract to the Bereaved. Tracts on Scepticism and Infidelity. Also, Books at 2d., 3d., 4d., 6d., and 1s. each. Children's Packets and Envelope ditto.
A large variety of Four-page Tracts, on tinted paper, with Woodcuts, from 6s. per 1000.

PARIS EXHIBITION. 1878.

The Committee of the MONTHLY TRACT SOCIETY, having secured a piece of ground immediately opposite the Trocadero Palace—the grand entrance to the Exhibition—intend to erect thereon a Kiosk, where illustrated Gospel Tracts and other religious publications, with portions of Holy Scripture in French, German, Italian, Spanish, and other languages, will be distributed and sold. At the Exhibition of 1867 the Society distributed nearly a million tracts in various languages, and they are able to state that much good attended that effort.

Contributions towards this undertaking are earnestly solicited, and will be thankfully received by Mr. JOHN STABB, 5, New Bridge Street, London, E.C., and by Mr. Sternberg, 28, Rue Mozart, Passy, Paris.

YOUNG MEN from the COUNTRY,
Who desire friends in London, recommendation to suitable lodgings, and information or counsel suited to their circumstances, will be welcomed at the

YOUNG MEN'S CHRISTIAN ASSOCIATION,
165, ALDERSGATE STREET, LONDON, E.C.,
Near the General Post Office.

CHRISTIAN YOUNG MEN COMING TO LONDON are invited on their arrival to unite in the fellowship by which the Members of the Association seek to strengthen each other in the confession of Christ, as well as to win other Young Men, their companions in business, to the service of the Redeemer.

MINISTERS, HEADS OF COMMERCIAL HOUSES, and PARENTS, are requested to commend Young Men in whom they are interested to the friendly attention of the Association. Branches exist in various parts of London, to which Young Men who are not settling in the Central District will be introduced by the Secretary.

The Members of the Association will be glad to show kindness to strangers, and to introduce them to the fellowship of Christian Churches, and to appropriate Christian work, as they may desire.

The arrangements, under the immediate superintendence of the Committee, are as follows:—

Bible Classes—Free to all Young Men.—Sunday Afternoon at 3.15; Tuesday Evening, 9.
Theological Class.—Monday Evening, 8.
Devotional Meetings and Addresses.—Thursday Evening, 6.30 and 9.
Prayer Meetings.—Sunday at 9.30 a.m.
LIBRARY, READING ROOMS, EDUCATIONAL CLASSES, LECTURES, &c., with all the conveniences of a Club (save dinners) are here, open to respectable Young Men on payment of a small Subscription.

Young Men, who may desire religious conversation and advice, will be cordially welcomed by the Officers of the Association.

W. EDWYN SHIPTON, *Secretary.*

The Religious Tract Society's Paris Depôt

IS AT

4, PLACE DU THÉÂTRE FRANÇAIS,

Where Tracts in the Principal European Languages may be obtained.

ILLUSTRATED BOOKS OF TRAVEL.

Imperial 8vo, 8s. each, elegantly bound, gilt edges.

1. **ENGLISH PICTURES, DRAWN WITH PEN AND PENCIL.** By the Rev. SAMUEL MANNING, LL.D., and the Rev. S. G. GREEN, D.D. With Coloured Frontispiece and numerous Wood Engravings.
"Next to seeing the beautiful places of the earth comes the delight of reading of them, and many a one who is doomed to begin and end his days within a 'cribb'd, cabined, and confined' circle, can roam guided by such a book, at the will of fancy, through sunny glades, by babbling streams, or over the breezy moorlands."—*The Times.*

2. **AMERICAN PICTURES, DRAWN WITH PEN AND PENCIL.** By the Rev. SAMUEL MANNING, LL.D. Profusely Illustrated in the best Style of Wood Engraving by Eminent English and Foreign Artists.
"These American Pictures are a credit to all concerned in their production."—*Pall Mall Gazette.* "A very interesting and entertaining volume."—*Spectator.* "Copiously and cleverly illustrated and pleasantly written."—*Daily News.*

3. **SWISS PICTURES, DRAWN WITH PEN AND PENCIL.** By the Rev. SAMUEL MANNING, LL.D. With numerous Illustrations, by Whymper and others.
"In this third edition there are so many additions and improvements that this beautiful volume is still more attractive and beautiful than ever."—*Standard.*

4. **"THOSE HOLY FIELDS."** Palestine. Illustrated by Pen and Pencil. By the Rev. SAMUEL MANNING, LL.D. Profusely Illustrated.
"The work is executed with great ability—but the great charm of the book is the illustrations. Very simple, but executed with extreme fidelity, and a thoroughly artistic feeling."—*Graphic.*

5. **THE LAND OF THE PHARAOHS.** Egypt and Sinai. Illustrated by Pen and Pencil. By the Rev. SAMUEL MANNING, LL.D. Profusely Illustrated with fine Engravings.
"Dr. Manning wields a lively and graceful pen. The volume is full of spirited and highly-finished engravings on wood."—*Standard.*
"Written in a pleasing, readable fashion. . . The woodcuts are capital."—*Athenæum.*

6. **ITALIAN PICTURES, DRAWN WITH PEN AND PENCIL.** By the Rev. SAMUEL MANNING, LL.D. Profusely Illustrated.
"The more we turn over the pages of this book, the more we like it. Italy is the theme of a great deal of fine writing and fine painting, but the plain descriptions and accurate drawings here really tell us more about it than a library of inspired poems and a gallery of ideal paintings."—*Times.*

7. **SPANISH PICTURES, DRAWN WITH PEN AND PENCIL.** By the Rev. SAMUEL MANNING, LL.D. With Illustrations by Gustave Doré and other eminent Artists.
"A volume that does credit to the writer and artists employed."—*Pall Mall Gazette.*
"The letter-press is pleasant reading, and many of the sketches are of the highest excellence."—*The Times.*

IN PREPARATION. *Uniform with the above Volumes.*

8. **FRENCH PICTURES, DRAWN WITH PEN AND PENCIL.**

Tracts in various foreign languages, at greatly reduced rates, may be obtained on application to the SECRETARIES, 56, Paternoster Row, London, E.C.

THE RELIGIOUS TRACT SOCIETY.

LONDON : 56, PATERNOSTER ROW ; 65, ST. PAUL'S CHURCHYARD ; AND 164, PICCADILLY.

GUIDE BOOKS.

The following Books can be obtained at any of the Offices of THOS. COOK & SON, or sent by Post to any part of the United Kingdom:—

Cook's Tourists' Guide to Holland, Belgium, and the Rhine. Price 3s. 6d. With Maps.

Cook's Tourists' Guide to Switzerland, showing all Routes to Paris, with descriptions of the places of interest. Price 3s. 6d. With Maps.

Cook's Tourists' Guide to the Black Forest. Price 3s. 6d. With Map.

New Guide to Ancient and Modern Rome. By SHAKSPERE WOOD. Price 6s. With Map. This work contains full Particulars of the recent Excavations in Rome.
"This is extremely well done. The information is clear and brief, given with judgment and good taste, and apparently exhaustive. It is hardly possible to conceive a more useful book for its especial purpose—that of guiding the hasty tourist to see as much as may be with the least expenditure of time."—*Guardian.*

Cook's Tourists' Guide to Northern Italy. Price 4s. With Maps.
"Cook's 'Northern Italy' will tell the traveller nearly all he wants to know of the chief cities of the North, including Florence, the approaches through the mountain passes from France, Switzerland, and Austria."—*Graphic.*

Cook's Tourists' Guide to Southern Italy. Price 4s. With Maps.
"Cook's 'Tourist Handbook to Southern Italy' is another of those plain, unpretending guides, which, like Cook's Coupons, are perhaps best suited for the inexperienced traveller, but to him will prove of more real service than the more voluminous and exhaustive manuals. It is as good a handbook as tourists can desire."—*Graphic.*

Cook's Handbook to Venice. Price 1s. With Plan.

Cook's Handbook to Florence. Price 1s. With Plan.
"Cook's Handbooks to Florence and Venice form two handy little volumes full of reliable information."—*John Bull.*

Cook's Handbook for Egypt, the Nile, and the Desert. Price 6s. With Five Maps.

Cook's Handbook for Palestine and Syria. Price 7s. 6d. With Four Maps.

A Few Words of Advice on Travelling and its Requirements. Addressed to Ladies. With Vocabulary in French and German and other useful information. Price 1s.

ADVERTISEMENTS.

GUIDE BOOKS, &c.—continued.

Cook's Guide to Paris and its Exhibition, 1878.
With Plan of Paris. Price 1s.

Cook's Handbook for London. Full particulars of all places of interest, Railways, Omnibuses, Tramways, Steamers, Cab Fares, Churches, Chapels, Public Buildings, National Institutions, Museums, Picture Galleries, Law Courts, Theatres, Clubs and Club Houses, Banks and Bankers in London, Short Excursions in the Suburbs, Hotels, &c., &c. With Two Maps. Price 6d.; cloth gilt, 1od. By post, 7d. and 1s.

Up the Nile by Steam. To the First and Second Cataracts. With Maps. Price 6d.

Programmes of Personally-Conducted and Independent Palestine Tours with extensions to **Egypt and the Nile.** With Maps. Price 6d.

Cook's Excursionist and Tourist Advertiser. Published at short intervals during the Season, in London, New York, and Brussels; and contains Programmes and Lists to the number of 1000 Specimen Tours; tickets for which are issued by THOS. COOK & SON, with Fares by every Route. Price 2d., or by Post 3d.

Cook's Continental Time-Tables and Tourists' Handbook. Contains the Time-Tables of the principal Continental Railway, Steamboat, and Diligence Companies, and includes EIGHT SECTIONAL MAPS, specially engraved; full directions as to Passports, Foreign Currency, etc. Compiled and arranged under the personal supervision of THOMAS COOK & SON. Price 1s.

Cook's Centennial Map of Atlantic Steamship Routes; and Tourists' Map of Central Europe. The two in cloth case. Price 9d.

LONDON: THOS. COOK & SON, LUDGATE CIRCUS, E.C.

WEST END AGENCY—Midland Railway Office, 445, West Strand
(opposite Charing Cross Station and Hotel).

BRANCH OFFICES:

BIRMINGHAM—Stephenson Place	GLASGOW—165, Buchanan Street
MANCHESTER—43, Piccadilly	PARIS—15, Place du Havre
LIVERPOOL—11, Ranelagh Street	COLOGNE—40, Domhof
LEEDS—1, Royal Exchange	BRUSSELS—22, Galerie du Roi
BRADFORD—Front of Midland Sta.	GENEVA—90, Rue du Rhone
SHEFFIELD—Change Alley Corner	ROME—1B, Piazza di Spagna
LEICESTER—63, Granby Street	CAIRO—Cook's Tourists' Pavilion,
DUBLIN—45, Dame Street	Shepheard's Hotel
EDINBURGH—9, Princes Street	JAFFA—Hotel Jerusalem

AMERICAN HOUSE—COOK, SON & JENKINS, 261, BROADWAY, NEW YORK.

COOK'S EXCURSIONS, TOURS,
AND
GENERAL TRAVELLING ARRANGEMENTS.

THOMAS COOK AND SON,

PIONEERS, Inaugurators, and Promoters of the principal systems of Tours established in Great Britain and Ireland, and on the Continent of Europe, are now giving increased attention to Ordinary Travelling Arrangements, with a view to rendering them as easy, practicable, and economical as circumstances will allow. During 37 years more than FIVE MILLIONS of Travellers have visited near and distant places under their arrangements; and their system of Tickets now provides for visiting the chief points of interest in the Four Quarters of the Globe.

Tourist Tickets by Midland Route issued by THOMAS COOK and SON to Derbyshire, Yorkshire, Lancashire, Morecambe Bay, Isle of Man, Scotland, Ireland, &c.; also Cheap Excursion Tickets to and from London.

Cook's English Lake Tours cover all points of Interest, including Windermere, Coniston, Ullswater, Derwentwater, Rydal, and Grasmere Lakes. Also Coaches and Carriage Excursions to visit all principal places.

Cook's West of England Tours, combining Railway, Coach, and Steamer to every point of interest between Bristol and the Land's End. The Tickets are prepared in Coupon form, and can be issued in combination, to meet the requirements of the Tourist. Hotel Coupons are also issued for First Class Hotels in the District.

Cook's Scotch Tours cover all points of Tourist interest in Scotland, Oban, Staffa, Iona, Isle of Skye, Caledonian Canal, Kyles of Bute, the Trossachs, the Highlands, the Lake District, Edinburgh, etc.; and can be used in a similar manner to the Irish Tours.

Cook's Irish Tours.—Thomas Cook and Son issue Tourist Tickets to and through all parts of Ireland, including the Giant's Causeway, Belfast, Dublin, Galway, Loch Erne, the Lakes of Killarney, etc. They can be used in connection with Tickets from London, or any town on the Midland Railway.

PARIS EXHIBITION.—See Special Programme issued by THOMAS COOK and SON.

Cook's Tickets to Paris are available by the Shortest and Cheapest Routes, and by Dover and Calais.

Cook's Swiss Tickets are available by every Route, and Cover every part of the Country. Thomas Cook and Son are the only Authorized Agents of every Swiss Railway, Steamboat, and Diligence Company. Every Alpine route is included in their arrangements.

Cook's Italian Tickets provide for every Route to and through Italy, and are offered at great Reductions in Fares.

Cook's Tours to Holland, Belgium, and the Rhine, are arranged upon a most comprehensive basis, Tickets being provided for every Route, for single and return journeys, and for Circular Tours. Breaks of journey are allowed at all places of interest.

Cook's Personally-conducted Tours have become a most popular feature in their arrangements. Parties are organized to leave London weekly during the season for Switzerland, Germany, Italy, and various parts of the Continent.

ADVERTISEMENTS. 117

COOK'S EXCURSIONS AND TOURS—*continued*.

The Steam Navigation of the Nile is committed by the Khedive Government entirely to **Thomas Cook and Son.** The Steamers (the only ones on the Nile) ply between Cairo and the First Cataract (600 miles), and the Second Cataract (810 miles). Tickets can be had, and Berths secured, at any of **Thomas Cook and Son's Offices.**

Tours to Palestine are rendered easy, safe, and economical, by the superior arrangements of **Thomas Cook and Son**, who now have their own Resident manager in Beyrout and Jaffa. They are therefore prepared to conduct large or small parties in the most comfortable manner through the country; to Jerusalem, the Dead Sea, the Jordan, Damascus, Sinai, etc. The parties can be so fixed as to go independently or under personal management any time between October and April. Nearly two thousand ladies and gentlemen have visited Palestine under their arrangements.

Turkey, Greece, the Levant, etc.—**Thomas Cook and Son** are now prepared to issue Tickets by any line of Steamers, to any port touched by the Austrian Lloyd's, Messageries Maritimes, and Rubattino Co.'s Steamers.

India, China, etc.—**Thomas Cook and Son** are the Agents of the principal Steamship Companies of the world, and are prepared to issue Tickets from Southampton, Venice, Ancona, Genoa, Naples, and Brindisi, to Alexandria, Aden, Bombay, Calcutta, Singapore, Hong Kong, Shanghai, or any other point in India or China.

Algerian Tours.—**Thomas Cook and Son** issue Tickets by any route to Algeria, and over the Algerian Railways and Diligence routes.

Norway, Sweden, and Denmark.—**Thomas Cook and Son** now issue Tourist Tickets by all principal Railways and Steamers for the most interesting parts of Scandinavia.

Round the World.—**Thomas Cook and Son** are prepared to issue a direct travelling Ticket for a journey Round the World by Steam, available to go either West or East. First Class, price £190.

Cook's Hotel Coupons, available at over four hundred first-class Hotels in various parts of the world, can be had by travellers purchasing **Cook's Tourist Tickets**, guaranteeing them first class accommodation at fixed and regular prices.

Passages to America and Canada are secured by **Thomas Cook and Son** for all the chief lines of Steamers. Arrangements are made for Tours through America, giving a choice of more than 200 Single and Tourist Tickets; and an Office has been opened in New York, under the joint arrangement of **Cook, Son, and Jenkins,** 261, Broadway.

Thomas Cook and Son's General Travelling Arrangements are so widely extended, that they can supply Tickets to almost any point that Tourists may wish to visit, in many cases at reductions, many ranging from twenty-five to forty-five per cent. below ordinary fares. The regular Travelling Ticket being issued in all cases printed in English on one side, and in the language of the country where it is used on the other, and it contains all the information the traveller needs.

Policies of Insurance against accidents of all kinds, by land and sea, are effected through the Office of **Thomas Cook and Son**, as Agents of the "Ocean, Railway, and General Accident Assurance Company, Limited."

Programmes can be had gratuitously, on application at the Offices of **Thomas Cook and Son**, or by post, in return for stamps covering postage.

Cook's Excursionist and Tourist Advertiser is published at short intervals during the season in London, New York, and Brussels, at 2d., post-free, 3d., and contains programmes and lists to the number of nearly one thousand specimen Tours. Tickets for which are issued by **Thomas Cook and Son**, with fares by every Route.

Cook's Continental Time Tables and Tourist Handbook, with Eight Sectional Maps, price 1s. Published monthly.

THOMAS COOK & SON,
Chief Office: Ludgate Circus, Fleet Street, London, E.C.
WEST-END AGENCY:
445, West Strand (opposite Charing Cross Station and Hotel).

J. GARDNER, SEN.,
Naturalist, &c.

BY APPOINTMENT TO HER MAJESTY THE QUEEN.

371, OXFORD STREET, LONDON, W. (ONLY),
(LATE OF 426).

NO CONNECTION WITH ANY OTHER HOUSE.

CENTRAL FIRE GUNS & RIFLES.

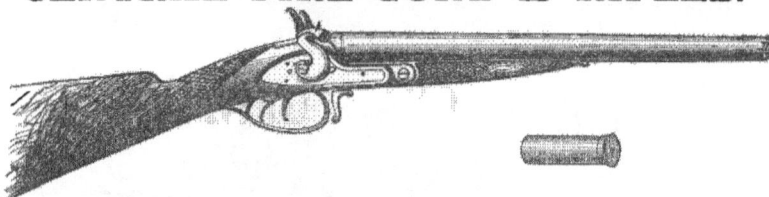

MESSRS. E. M. REILLY & CO.,
MANUFACTURERS OF GUNS, RIFLES, & REVOLVERS,
By Special Appointment to H.M. the King of Portugal,

Have ready for delivery a large assortment of the above, comprising the latest and most approved patterns.

"SELF-EXTRACTING HAMMERLESS" GUN commands attention; also several other patterns which can be recommended.

EXPRESS DOUBLE RIFLES, for all kinds of shooting, carrying heavy charges of powder. Makers of the LARGE BORE RIFLES used by Sir Samuel Baker and H. M. Stanley, Esq., and other great travellers.

Sportsmen and others will find, at our case in the Exhibition, every description of Arms suited to their wants.

PRICE LISTS ON APPLICATION.

502 AND 315, OXFORD STREET, LONDON,
AND
RUE SCRIBE, PARIS.

HOPE BROTHERS,
TAILORS AND GENERAL OUTFITTERS,
44 & 46, Ludgate Hill, 1, Old Bailey, and 282, High Holborn,
LONDON.

Travellers requiring any article of Gentlemen's Dress will find at this Establishment a large and well selected Stock to select from, at moderate prices.

In the Tailoring and Shirt Making Departments the best cutters and workmen only are employed. A good fit is guaranteed, and any article not approved of may be exchanged or the money returned.

All Goods are marked in plain figures, for Cash only.

PALAIS ROYAL GARDENS.

ANGLO-AMERICAN RESTAURANT

A. MERCIER,
PROPRIETOR.

BREAKFASTS, LUNCHEONS, AND DINNERS
AT MODERATE PRICES.

LARGE & SMALL ROOMS FOR PRIVATE PARTIES.
LADIES' PRIVATE TOILET ROOM.

36, GALERIE MONTPENSIER, & 24, RUE MONTPENSIER.

ARTIST AND PHOTOGRAPHER.

M. ALOPHE

25, RUE ROYALE (Close to the Madeleine)

FIVE MINUTES FROM THE PLACE DU HAVRE,

PARIS.

OIL PICTURES, WATER COLOUR, CRAYONS, ENAMELS

In the Latest Style.

REPRODUCTIONS, ENLARGEMENTS, &c.

ENGLISH SPOKEN.

THE BEST, LIGHTEST, & MOST PERFECT
LOCK-STITCH SEWING MACHINES ARE THE

MANUFACTURED BY THE
WANZER SEWING MACHINE CO., Limited,
PRICE LISTS FREE.
4, GT. PORTLAND STREET, REGENT CIRCUS, LONDON.
131, BOULEVARD SEBASTOPOL, PARIS.

SAMUEL COOMBES,
MANUFACTURING CARVER & GILDER,
DEALER IN WORKS OF ART,
(Established 1832)
331, STRAND, LONDON, W.C.
IMMEDIATELY OPPOSITE SOMERSET HOUSE.

Old Frames Re-gilt, Oil Paintings Skilfully Cleaned and Repaired.

ENGRAVINGS CLEANED AND RESTORED.
N.B.—A large Collection of High-class Paintings & Water-colour Drawings on View.

NO MORE SLEEPLESS NIGHTS,
HUNTER'S SOLUTION OF CHLORAL,
PAIN, THE WORLD-WIDE REMEDY FOR SLEEP,
SEA-SICKNESS, TOOTHACHE, NEURALGIA, &c.
Surpassing everything hitherto discovered.
THE BEST PATENT MEDICINE OF THE DAY.
Of all Chemists, 1s. 1½d., 2s. 9d., 4s. 6d.; from J. Hunter, Kensington, Three Stamps extra.

NOTICE TO TRAVELLERS.

Accidental Death or Injuries of all Kinds
INSURED AGAINST BY THE
OCEAN, RAILWAY, & GENERAL ACCIDENT ASSURANCE AND GUARANTEE COMPANIES, LIMITED.
HEAD OFFICES:—MANSION HOUSE BUILDINGS, LONDON.

EMPOWERED BY SPECIAL ACT OF PARLIAMENT.

Tickets covering the risk of travelling by any kind of conveyance throughout Europe may be had at any of THOS. COOK & SON'S Offices.

£1,000 available for One Month ... Premium 5/-
£500   ,,   ,,   ...   ,,   3/-
£200   ,,   ,,   ...   ,,   1/6
£1,000 available for Three Months ...   ,,   10/-
£500   ,,   ,,   ...   ,,   5/-
£200   ,,   ,,   ...   ,,   2/6

General Accident Policies.
£1,000 available for Twelve Months ... Premium 25/-

Railway Policies for Risks in the United Kingdom.
£1,000 available for Twelve Months ... Premium 7/6
Throughout Europe ... 10/-

Double these Premiums secure a Weekly Allowance of 10/- for every £100 assured in cases of Disablement.

Accidents at Sea.
POLICIES TO OR FROM ANY PORT IN THE WORLD AT VERY LOW RATES.

GUARANTEE POLICIES ISSUED TO PERSONS IN SITUATIONS OF TRUST.

POLICIES ISSUED AT THE OFFICES OF THE COMPANY,
AND BY
THOS. COOK & SON, LUDGATE CIRCUS; and 445, WEST STRAND, LONDON.

BIRMINGHAM—Stephenson Place.
MANCHESTER—43, Piccadilly.
LIVERPOOL—11, Ranelagh Street.
LEEDS—1, Royal Exchange.
BRADFORD—Front of Midland Station.
SHEFFIELD—Change Alley Corner.
DUBLIN—45, Dame Street.
EDINBURGH—9, Princes Street.

GLASGOW—165, Buchanan Street.
PARIS—15, Place du Havre.
COLOGNE—40, Domhof.
BRUSSELS—22, Galerie du Roi.
GENEVA—90, Rue du Rhone.
ROME—1b, Piazza di Spagna.
NEW YORK—261, Broadway.

WHY DOES HAIR FALL OFF?

From many causes. Sometimes from local disturbing agencies, such as sickness; sometimes from neglect in cleansing; but more frequently from decay in the saps and tissues which supply each individual hair. In such case,

OLDRIDGE'S
BALM OF COLUMBIA

Is an excellent corrective of the many insidious sources of decay which ruin nature's chief ornament.

It stimulates, strengthens, and increases the growth of Hair; softens and nourishes it when grown; and arrests its decline. Besides this, it acts on those pigments the constant supply of which is essential to the Hair retaining its colour.

The Hair of the Head & the Whiskers & Moustachios

Are alike benefited. For children it is invaluable, as it forms the basis of a magnificent Head of Hair, prevents Baldness in mature age, and obviates the use of dyes and poisonous restoratives.

ESTABLISHED UPWARDS OF SIXTY YEARS.
(*A sufficient guarantee of its efficacy.*)

Sold by all Perfumers and Chemists at 3s. 6d., 6s., and 11s. only. Wholesale and Retail by the Proprietors,

C. & A. OLDRIDGE,
22, WELLINGTON STREET, STRAND, LONDON, W.C.

BALM OF COLUMBIA.
ESTABLISHED UPWARDS OF SIXTY YEARS.

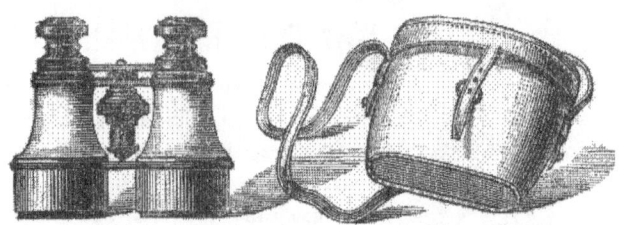

NEGRETTI & ZAMBRA,

TOURIST'S SCIENTIFIC REQUISITES

Opticians and Meteorological Instrument Makers

To **HER MAJESTY THE QUEEN** *and the Government Departments,*

HOLBORN VIADUCT;

Also at 45, CORNHILL ; 122, REGENT ST.; and CRYSTAL PALACE, SYDENHAM.

	£	s.	d.
* Pocket Barometer, to foretell Weather	3	3	0
* Ditto, with Scale of Altitudes for correctly ascertaining the Height of Mountains ... £5 5s. 0d. and	6	6	0
* Tourist's Binocular Glasses ... £2 2s. 0d. and	3	3	0
* Negretti and Zambra's New Binocular—			
Prices in Bronze, with Leather Sling Case	5	5	0
Ditto, in Aluminium	9	9	0

The New Binocular is specially designed for Field or Military Service. It is strong in Frame, and of little weight, and can be used with one hand ; Optically, it is of high power ; gives a large field of view, abundance of light, perfect definition; and achromatic, so that any Colour or Flag can be recognized at long distances.

A Glass, to be really useful, should possess mechanical strength, optical perfection, and be handy either on foot or in the saddle; these qualities are pre-eminently united in the NEW BINOCULAR.

	£	s.	d.
* Tourist's Telescopes, 15 to 20 miles' range £4 4s. 0d. to	5	5	0
* Pedometers, for Measuring Walking Distances ...	3	3	0

* *These are to be obtained at* THOS. COOK & SON'S *Office, Ludgate Circus.*

THOS. COOK & SON'S
FOREIGN BANKING & MONEY EXCHANGE DEPARTMENT.

Chief Office—LUDGATE CIRCUS, LONDON, E.C.

Foreign Monies Exchanged at most Advantageous Rates. Drafts and Circular Notes Issued and Cashed.

Messrs. THOS. COOK & SON have added the above Department to their old-established Tourist business, in order to more fully meet the requirements of their numerous patrons.

LEICESTER.
COOK'S
COMMERCIAL and FAMILY TEMPERANCE HOTEL,
63, GRANBY STREET,
(ADJOINING THE TEMPERANCE HALL).

LADIES and GENTLEMEN visiting Leicester, for purposes of Business or Pleasure, will find at this Establishment the ordinary comforts of a quiet home, in close proximity to the chief centres of commerce. The Hotel is situated in the principal thoroughfare, within five minutes' walk of the Railway Station, and about an equal distance from the principal Banks, Public Offices, Mercantile Establishments, Markets, Post Office, &c. An Ordinary is provided daily at One o'clock.

PHRENOLOGY.

PROF. and MRS. DR. FOWLER (of New York) give PHRENOLOGICAL AND PHYSIOLOGICAL CONSULTATIONS DAILY, in their Rooms, in Cook's New Building, 107, Fleet Street, from 10 a.m. to 5 p.m.

WILLIAM SHINGLETON,

Tailor

AND HABIT MAKER,

60,

NEW BOND STREET,

LONDON.

A LARGE SELECTION OF THE BEST AND NEWEST GOODS AT THE LOWEST CASH PRICES.

TOURIST'S SUITS . from £3 3s.
TROUSERS . . . from 16s.

NO CREDIT GIVEN.

SAMPSON & CO.,

SOLE MAKERS OF THE

SURPLICE SHIRT.

Six for 45s., 51s.

*COLOURED FRENCH CAMBRIC. All New Patterns.
SURPLICE SHIRTS.   6 for 45s.
SARATTA GAUZE.   Suitable for Travelling.
SURPLICE SHIRTS.   6 for 45s.
FLANNEL SHIRTS.   Made from Undyed Wool.
SURPLICE SHIRTS.   Warranted Shrunk.

Detailed Priced Outfit Lists and Self-Measurement Cards sent on application.

TAILORING DEPARTMENT.

Homespun Trousers, 16s., 21s.
Tweed or Angola Trousers, 25s., 30s.
Homespun Suits, 63s., 70s.
Diagonal Cloth Morning Coat and Waistcoat, 75s., 90s.
Blue Serge Suits, 63s., 70s.

TERMS:—ALL GOODS MARKED IN PLAIN FIGURES. CASH, 5 PER CENT. DISCOUNT.

SAMPSON & CO.,
Hosiers, Glovers, India and Colonial Outfitters,
130, OXFORD STREET,
NEAR HOLLES STREET, LONDON, W.

www.ingramcontent.com/pod-product-compliance
Lightning Source LLC
Chambersburg PA
CBHW022139160426
43197CB00009B/1347